This book of memories is dedicated
to my daughter Lydia,
hoping that she will have as many happy memories
of her childhood as I did.

INTRODUCTION

Was it only yesterday that I was so young, with boundless energy scrambling over Whiston School wall and down the field to the brook? Looking up - watching the wind blowing over the fields of long summer grass in a waving motion mimicking the sea.

All the windows were glowing afire in the cottages which made up this Moorlands village reflecting back the glowing redness of the setting sun. A few fleeting moments which for some reason or other stay in your memory forever.

This story is taken from the memories of a young impressionable moorlands lad who found an enduring friendship with two country women who lived at the top of Whiston village.

Although set in the late 1950s and 1960s, it is already a story of a vanished way of life and of characters lost as mere echoes in the roaring winds of the moorland hills.

A bleak house, in a bleak village perched high in the North Staffordshire hills - The House on the Plain.

JOHN WILLIAMS
Dilhorne 1996

ACKNOWLEDGEMENTS

Thank you!

Sincere thanks go to the following people;
Jeanette Cheadle for typing the book;
Janet Williams for proof reading;
David Williams for helping recall some of the memories,
my mother-in-law for supplying some of the photographs,
my daughter, Lydia, for trudging around Whiston through the snow in
the winter taking photographs, and also helping me with the
illustrations, to which also Owen Griffith's significant contribution;
Mr & Mrs B.H. Chalfant from the U.S.A. for their encouragement;
Owen Griffiths, George Short, George Bowyer, G.M.Fisher, and
Annie and Herbert Bull, for the use of photographs

- and my wife for putting up with my hours of 'scribbling'.

Whiston Copper Works which closed in 1890

The demolition and removal of stone to build Whiston Church

CHAPTER 1
Delving into History

I have always enjoyed the subject of history and reading biographies of peoples' lives through the ages - perhaps this is why I wanted to record the social history of my own younger days whilst they are still fresh in my mind. I have often wished that as a young lad I had taken notes of the many stories retold to me by a grand old Staffordshire Moorlands lady who lived for most of her exceptionally long life in the village of Whiston. Whiston was a village, so she said, that when God created the world he made last - and forgot to finish it!

Alas! When you are young, so much is forgotten in the freshness of life, when all lies in front of you. She told me many stories of her experiences, funny stories, sad stories, but all tales of a life very far removed from my own modern times. But I was at an age when you are not too concerned about the lives of yesterday's fossilised generation.

Although this is not a story of her life, I felt it important to give you an overview of her eventful life as a preamble to my own story. I had better introduce you to the lady in question then. Her name was Mrs Harriet Finney-Elks, but known as Mrs Finney to generations of Whiston folk.

This old lady, (for she always seemed so), belonged to a vanished Edwardian age, a time of a well-ordered society where, particularly in country parts, the Lord of the Manor still dominated village community life, where hats would be doffed in his presence, forelocks touched, curtseys bobbed and heads bowed as he passed by.

She had brought this Edwardian age with her. Here it was in her own house. Her furniture - carpets, pictures, tapestries, china and ornaments - all came from this and previous reigns. It was as if you had stepped back in time. Perhaps many Moorlands cottages and farmsteads could boast the same but something here was different. Was it because she so rarely left her house or Whiston village that here was to be found a haven of good manners, a well ordered lifestyle and a timeless atmosphere somehow moth-balled and stored away like some Brigadoon, not in Scotland, but here in the North Staffordshire hills?

Mrs Finney had a daughter, named Dorothy. She had jet black hair, dark skin and a very distinctive laugh. Dorothy was very practical and kind, but sometimes with a sharpness which meant that she stood for no nonsense and spoke with a plain directness which is a trait found in people from the Moorlands. Dorothy, as you will discover in the coming chapters led a 'normal' fairly hard life - but a life which was later eased by modern conveniences.

So then, who was Mrs Finney? Let us look back together briefly of how she came to Whiston - and for those who don't know the village, we will have just a little of its history.

My brother Ken with Dorothy and Mrs Finney, who is seated
with 'Romp' the dog in 1969

CHAPTER 2
Mrs Finney

Mrs Finney was born Harriet Bull in 1896, high in the North Staffordshire Moorland Hills, her family having originated in the Elkstones area, near to the Derbyshire border. The Bull family had lived in this wild area for generations. The family moved to a cottage at Windy Harbour, Upper Cotton, set high on a ridge with unparalleled views south over the entire county. The cottage had once been part of a brick kiln business using local clay to manufacture bricks for new housing different to the traditional gritstone cottages of the centuries before.

Windy Harbour is justly called as there is little to stop the roaring winds blowing from the East and North in winter. Here was the homestead where Harriet was brought up with her sisters Olive,

Harriet's parents sat outside Brickyard House at Windy Arbour

Emma and Alice, and her brothers. Harriet's sister Emma would continue to live at Windy Harbour all her long life until her recent death.

Harriet very nearly didn't survive her childhood, she almost drowned when she tried to examine her fringe in the pool of water near the house where in times past the clay had been taken for brick manufacture. She fell into the water and was very lucky not to drown.

Into Service

Like many young girls, there was not too many options when it came to earning a living. Most either went into 'service' with large families, worked on farms or ended up working in the factories in the town of Leek, famous for its weaving and fabric dyeing. Harriet opted for service as a maid, leaving her family and friends at the age of thirteen, to take up the arduous duties of an under-house maid to an important local family in their stone-built manor house, Whiston Eaves, just outside the village of Whiston.

The family to which Harriet became maid was the Smith family, Lords of the Manor of Whiston, since the early 1790s and owners of much of the surrounding countryside, farms and woodland. The Smiths then were very important gentry to the local community. Their Manor House had been rebuilt just after 1800 and was called grandly 'Whiston Eaves'.

The hamlet of Whiston Eaves could be found by taking the Eaves Lane route from Whiston to Oakamoor. It was set in beautiful woodlands leading down to the Churnet Valley and was a solidly built house with pleasant lawns of modest size, befitting the Squire of Whiston. Just how long a house had stood at Eaves' is unknown. We know that the Smith family rebuilt it soon

A shooting party at Whiston Eaves Hall with Dr Geoff Hall's father fifth from the left

after purchasing the Manor from Old Squire Brindley who died in Trentham in 1806.

Old Squire Brindley had sold much of the estate around Whiston at a sale in 1797 which included some large local farms such as Eavesfford, later lost to the estate when bankruptcy threatened the Smith family early in Queen Victoria's reign. The Brindleys had held a house and Manor at Eaves since the 1480s having moved from the Bradnop area near to the town of Leek. They were related to the Brindleys who owned estates and farms in that area including the famous canal engineer's father - James Brindley.

Well! Enough of this digression into history, back then to Harriet and her years as a maid in Edwardian society! Being a maid at the Big House' was a very hard job, especially for a young girl of thirteen years old. She was up very early, 4.30 am every morning to clear the ashes from the previous day's fires, remake fires in the kitchen, parlour and drawing room and wash the coal for the brass coal scuttles (strange but true, coal was washed so that it was clean for house use).

She had to ensure that enough hot water was available for the Master and Mistress's use in their morning baths. She then had to help prepare the table for breakfast, help to serve breakfast, clear things away, help her ladyship in her preparations for the day, then clean and polish all day long, along with many other tasks added to the daily toil! No wonder she was ready for an early bedtime - exhausted no doubt!

This was, of course, no different than the life experienced by thousands of Harriets up and down the country and many were treated much more harshly than she was. The Smiths, although firm, were good employers - many of the old Whiston folk I was to know when I was young had worked for them at some time in their lives.

One early admonishment Harriet received was for the over zealous cleaning of Mrs Smith's prized collection of antique silver, whilst Mrs Smith was out! Oh dear, Harriet! This turned out not to be silver but very old, antique pewter from the time before the civil war, bought from Squire Brindley!

It seems that pewter should never be cleaned.

11

Harriet had polished away all the grime and patina of the centuries until it sparkled. All the hard work was examined with abject horror by the mistress - and shock, horror and tearing of hair! The damage was done however and Harriet now in tears was very much in disgrace. She lived to clean another day and grew to enjoy her life with the Smiths.

Occasional visits out to Leek or Cheadle, nearby market towns, broke the pattern of drudgery of a housemaid's life and a visit to the Earl of Shrewsbury's Alton Towers made a lasting impression on young Harriet. She was to return there in the 1920s for the great sale of furniture and effects at the Shrewsbury Sale. She became the proud owner of several vases and pieces of china which she kept in pride of place in her bedroom along with the sale catalogue which I would read with wonder!

Looking at Harriet and listening to her stories, it was hard to imagine her as a maid now in later years when she led a life far removed from those early days. Perhaps something of the Smith's lifestyle rubbed off on her?

Harriet's life as a maid was cut tragically short by an attack of rheumatic fever, which she blamed on a trip to Leek in an open carriage in winter, getting both wet and very cold - however else it was caught. She soon became very ill and was sent home where she was not expected to live. Harriet was made of sterner stuff and she lived, but with a weak heart and constitution, which meant that she would never work again.

Living back at Windy Harbour, Harriet spent the next few years never expecting to live a normal life. She became very close to the family of Doctor Hall, a medical doctor from Waterhouses, a village but a few miles distant from Windy Harbour, situated on the main road from Leek to Ashbourne.

By direction of the Executors of the late Earl of Shrewsbury and Talbot

CATALOGUE

OF THE

VALUABLE CONTENTS

OF

ALTON TOWERS

STAFFORDSHIRE

which will be sold by auction
on the premises by Messrs.

W. S. BAGSHAW & SONS

ON

Tuesday, January 15th, 1924

AND THE TEN FOLLOWING DAYS (except Saturday, 19th,
and Monday, 28th)

at 11.30 a.m. prompt each day

Solicitors :

Messrs. McLeod, Eyre, Dowling & Co., 1, Lincoln's Inn Fields, W.C. 2

Auction Offices :

UTTOXETER, ASHBOURNE AND DERBY

Telephone No. 44 Uttoxeter   Telegrams: "Bagshaw", Uttoxeter"

Harriet did quite a lot of baby sitting for the Halls, she was often nursemaid to young Geoff, and in return they allowed her to use their dog-cart for trips to Whiston. She always remarked that long before she got to Whiston it was possible to see the massive chimney of the copper works in the distance.

Life changed dramatically for Harriet when she met and married John (Jack) Finney-Elks of Whiston. After a brief courtship they were married in Whiston on the 5th April 1926. One the same day her life-long friend and near neighbour Mrs Kent was also married.

There was a large family gathering at Whiston for the wedding and afterwards at Windy Harbour. Generations from both sides of the family are on the wedding photograph. Relations travelled from Oulton, Shrewsbury, Fradswell and from the Moorland Hills.

Harriet had two charming bridesmaids; her cousin from Oulton, near Stone, Mary Malpass, and Harriet's sister Emma. All looked so very elegant in their 1920s costumes. I have included photographs of their wedding day on the following page. Harriet and Jack were both 30 years old when they married and went to live in Willow Cottage, Black Lane, Whiston, just around the corner from Jack's mother and father who lived in Finney Row.

Dorothy and her cousins Annie and John Bull outside of their Auntie Emma's house at Windy Harbour

The wedding of John Finney to Harriet Bull in 1926. Harriet's sister Emma, who lived in the family house at Windy Harbour all her life is on the far right of the picture. Mary Malpass, her cousin from Oulton, is on the left.

A family wedding photograph taken at Windy Harbour - Finneys, Bulls, Malpasses and many village friends

CHAPTER 3
The Finney Family

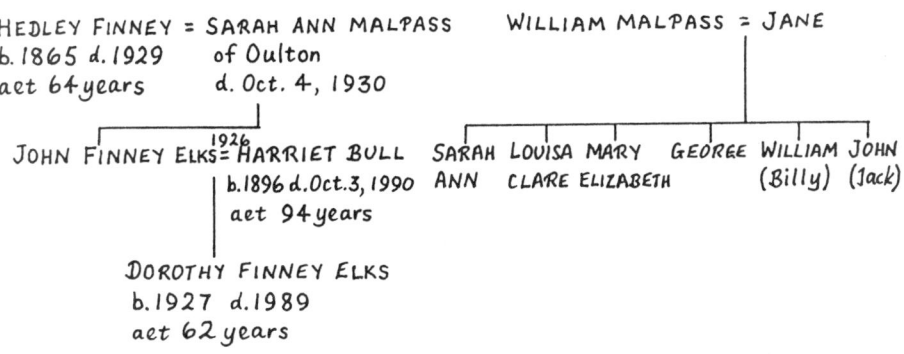

HEDLEY FINNEY = SARAH ANN MALPASS   WILLIAM MALPASS = JANE
b. 1865 d. 1929   of Oulton
aet 64 years   d. Oct. 4, 1930

JOHN FINNEY ELKS = HARRIET BULL   SARAH LOUISA MARY   GEORGE WILLIAM JOHN
1926   b.1896 d.Oct.3, 1990   ANN CLARE ELIZABETH   (Billy) (Jack)
    aet 94 years

DOROTHY FINNEY ELKS
b. 1927 d. 1989
aet 62 years

The Finney's were proud to be a branch of one of the oldest families in Staffordshire, a family who could trace their roots back to 1066, when they accompanied William of Normandy in the conquest of England.

The original family name was FENIS and like many names was corrupted over the centuries to Fynney and latterly to Finney. Any family which can trace its roots back to the conquest has many branches, but the Staffordshire Moorlands had always been their main base. Harriet told me that Jack's family had originated in the village down the Churnet Valley

Oakamoor

15

The row of cottages which were called "Finney Row"

Sneyd Arms

below Whiston called Oakamoor, home to another famous Brass and Copper works. The family had moved to Whiston village to live right under the shadow of another mighty copper works, this one operated by a man named Keys whose family had been brought over from Germany to work at the world famous 18th century Cheadle Brass Works. Keys ended up buying the Whiston Copper Works from the Duke of Devonshire. The bleak works polluted the air and fields around Whiston, creating huge slag heaps and left a legacy of poisoned land for years after its closure in 1890.

The Finney's lived in a row of stone built cottages next to the oldest hostelry in Whiston, the Ship Inn. Their small back gardens were right under the walls of the old works until 1907 when the empty and redundant works was demolished and the stone sold to build the new church in the village, St.Mildreds.

Jack Finney's father, Hedley Finney, born in 1865, had married a girl from the seemingly far off village of Oulton, near Stone, Staffordshire. The girls name was Sarah-Ann Malpass. I often wonder how they came to meet, but meet they did, and fell in love and married.

Sarah-Ann came to Whiston on a cart, piled high with all the choicest

Hedley and Sarah

furniture taken from her family home, a fact resented by her sisters at the time and then even by the next generation too!

I would sit listening to this story related by Harriet, who would list the pieces of furniture Sarah had brought with her - how on earth they managed to get a heavy cart load of antique furniture up the steep incline of Whiston Bank I cannot imagine. She must have dearly loved him to leave the idyllic village of Oulton for the cold, northern Moorland village of Whiston!

Towards the end of their life together they saw Jack married to Harriet and their grand daughter, Dorothy, born in 1927. Sadly, Hedley became acutely depressed, finally losing his life in a shotgun accident in his cottage in 1929. Sarah, his wife, died a year later in 1930. Perhaps the great economic 'Slump' has something to do with it?

Dorothy was the apple of her father's eye. But unfortunately, her mother, always a semi-invalid, then suffered from cancer and major cancer surgery to combat the disease. Once again Harriet survived but the cards were heavily stacked against Dorothy ever having a life of her own choosing, due to the invalidity of her mother.

The family moved the short distance to the more spacious 5, The Plain, Whiston which had land - an orchard, a large garden, and its own well.

Dorothy did have some romance in her life. When she was young, there was a very talented artist from Leek, who drew a magnificent picture of Dorothy's dog Nellie which was framed and hung in her bedroom.

At a party held to celebrate Dorothy's 21st

Dorothy

Dorothy's 21st Birthday

birthday in 1948, her father in his speech made it quite clear that Dorothy could never be spared or released from her duty to her invalid mother. It was a message that she would not be free to marry. As a dutiful daughter, Dorothy's fate was set. Her father died painfully of cancer in 1950 and left Dorothy to carry on alone.

Dorothy was denied a life of her own, but how much bitterness did she feel? It surfaced occasionally, but Dorothy bore it well and no one could blame her for her sometimes sharp nature. A small cast of people helped her through her life and as Harriet survived her 80s and on into her 90s everyone wondered what Dorothy would do with a life of her own when her mother passed on.

Sadly this was not to be known. Dorothy suffered with cancer herself which also at the same time took her cousin John Bull, her closest relative. Dorothy died in the Douglas MacMillan Home in Stoke-on-Trent in 1989 aged only 62 years. Her funeral service was packed with many friends and family in the Chapel in Whiston which she loved dearly.

Harriet Finney, not expected to live into her 20s, died in the following year, 1990, aged an incredible 94 years!

Harriet and Jack in Whiston in the late 1920s

Cheadle High Street in the 1950s

CHAPTER 4
Leaving Whiston

Being born in the Moorlands village of Whiston, it has always had a special place in my heart and in my youth, it was a place I loved to be in. My first seven years were spent growing up in Whiston, going to the village school which was a very pleasant experience, making friends their, going to the Chapel Sunday School and visiting many of the village folk with my mother. Then in my seventh year my family moved to the nearby town of Cheadle, which in the late 1950s was really quite small, but compared to Whiston seemed a vast metropolis!

Janet and I at the Townend shop in Cheadle 1961

It meant leaving everything I had grown to love - a country society, my friendly village school, the chance to run in open fields, watch nature, enjoy village friends, a large garden and a wonderful view. We moved to a small house with a small garden on what was then the edge of the town. There was really nothing to say against Cheadle; before its great expansion it still had an attractive shopping centre and was set in attractive countryside. But to a lad used to the open air life in the Moorlands it was a depressing prospect.

It seemed that I had left my happy life behind, for although Whiston was only five miles away from Cheadle, it seemed as if it was a hundred. Trying to settle in at the local primary school was a painful experience. So many children, all who had friends of their own. As a new boy I was, after all, an alien to be picked on and fought with. It was all quite a shock which took a long time to recover from.

Little wonder then that I escaped back into the hills whenever I could where I would find friendship, freedom, solitude and adventure.

Whiston has also gone through enormous changes from that small village of the late 1950s. It is a different community - in fact a whole way of life and people has passed away into mere memories. These memories were recorded in my mind and as so much social-historical information is never put down, and in time is lost for ever, I would like to share them with you now - and not wait for old age!

Carting the stone away from Whiston Copper Works

The reason I was able to return to Whiston so often was my close family friendship with Mrs Harriet Finney and her daughter Dorothy. I think that all my family enjoyed visiting what became known as Dorothy's; certainly my elder brother David was a regular visitor to Dorothy's before I was allowed to visit there myself.

Dorothy and her Mother, Harriet, who lived as I have said at 5 The Plain, Whiston, situated at the very top of Whiston village near to the blackened, brooding Whiston Hall, which in those days stared out blankly over the heather-covered and rocky Common. Its windows were blocked to the light by the surrounding tall black trees which housed a giant rookery. The constant cawing and wheeling of the birds around their nests added to the air of mystery which with my fertile imagination enhanced the stories of the former owners of the Hall and Copper Works both of which had left so many scars in the village. It was the sort of place that the Bronte Sisters or Jane Austen would have been proud to write a tragic novel about!

Unlike today, this part of the village was very quiet, before the days when Whiston Hall was opened up as a golf centre and the Common tamed; the constant coming and going of cars, the golf balls whistling over your head. It was altogether a different atmosphere from today.

The Common as it was then, was a good place to explore, have adventures, walk with Dorothy's dog, climb the enormous slab of stone set in the fields, search out the walled orchard, climb the rocks, breathe the fresh, cold, northern air and wonder at the breathtaking views with the patchwork of gritstone walls, trees and woods. How many happy hours did I spend roaming over these fields, with Toby the dog and a bag of pear drops? This was all the company I needed, the feeling of being close to nature - trees instead of people, a dog instead of friends, a whistling wind instead of the roar of traffic, stonewalls instead of rows of houses, sheep, cows, birds, rabbits and never seeing a soul; and then back to Dorothy's which was also a world in itself as I intend you to find out!

There was nowhere for me which could compare with Whiston.

In the front garden in 1960. I am with my younger sister Janet and Toby. Standing in front of the house are my father and Mrs Finney.

A side view of Whiston Hall, taken from the entrance of Dorothy's cornfield

The Cheadle Bus standing at the monument in Leek

CHAPTER 5
Getting to Whiston on the Bus

Getting to Whiston village from Cheadle was not as easy as you might think in those days and to a young lad it was rather an adventure in itself. Although Whiston is only five miles from Cheadle, there was no direct bus service with the exception of a round service to Cheadle market each Friday and a circular service on Saturday which took you through Froghall and Foxt before Whiston and then back to Cheadle. It was possible to catch a Leek-bound bus, getting off at Froghall but this meant a walk up the very steep, notorious Whiston Bank (also known as Froghall Bank) across the Plain, an old disused limestone tram track, over Lees Heath, into the village centre known as Brookhollow, then up another steep hill which was the ancient roadway through the village before the coming of the Turnpike through Whiston, known as Big Road. This old lane was known as Black Lane or Back Lane each name being quite plausible - Black Lane owing to the proximity of the belching copper works which blackened all the village buildings including Whiston Hall and poisoned the land around until it closed in 1896 - or Back Lane as it was the back way around the village. It was Back Lane in the early 1970s when I returned to live in the village, but it has now reverted to being Black Lane!

Being tied to school during the week, except in the long summer holidays of six weeks, meant that it was often only on a Saturday that I could make the journey to Whiston. I would catch the bus from Cheadle to Froghall, Foxt Village then on to Whiston, getting off the bus at the Pinfold where Black Lane joined the main turnpike road. It was then a short walk along the lane until the roof top of Dorothy's came into view and my day's adventure could begin in earnest.

    The journey I enjoyed most, however, was on a Wednesday when many Moorland villagers made their way to the important markets held in Leek, a pleasant town, which in those days had cobbled streets, many of which have since been covered in tarmac. The bus would leave Cheadle with few spare seats, heading for the village of Oakamoor, climbing upwards to the ridge known as High Shutt which still had an ancient tree which was a landmark for miles around. Then following the woodland road, past Hawksmoor, a nature reserve, and following the wooded slopes down into the Churnet Valley to the busy industrial village of Oakamoor, set by the river Churnet. At that time Oakamoor looked very different, as it was still home to the copperworks of Thomas Boltons - a mass of buildings and chimneys, some dating back to the days of Patten, whose brass works made Cheadle famous throughout the world in the 18th and 19th centuries. Cheadle brass was then the finest in the world.

Although the Cheadle works was long gone, the Oakamoor works was still working its last days before the whole works was closed and the manufacture moved up the valley to Froghall in 1963. Many years previously my maternal great-grandfather had been in charge of the steam engines at

Oakamoor so I always felt an empathy with the place.

Oakamoor was prone to flooding which made it a precarious place to invest in modern factory buildings so the whole industrial complex was demolished. The scars would soon heal, leaving a picturesque village in an idyllic setting with a large picnic site where the smoky, noisy factory once was, its tall chimney dominating the scene and sending smoke and fumes down the valley. Picking up extra passengers in the village centre, the bus began to climb out of Oakamoor, up out of the valley towards my destination - Whiston. There always seemed to be a good

Smokeamoor - Oakamoor Works

26

many women on the bus, all armed with empty shopping bags and full purses which of course would be crammed full of shopping on their return from Leek.

Getting the bus out of Oakamoor on the next leg of its journey was no easy task. It began the slow whining crawl up the steep Carr Bank, a twisting turning road which climbed up the hillside. This was a time for the nervous to hold their breath (I was one of them), as the bus began to shudder, going slower and slower - jokes were exchanged about running backwards to Oakamoor! This never happened as the bus would crash its gears and lurch forward for the final pull out of the valley, leaving behind the lush, beautiful wooded hillside and nestling village below for the pasture and woodland of Moneystone with its stone-built farms dotting the countryside. This is where a new sand works would later rip apart this beautiful part of the world in search of the valuable white silica sand.

The countryside changes as the road to Whiston rises higher, leaving the woodlands and pleasant valley for fields of irregular shape, edged with sandstone walls and small farmsteads with trees planted to protect them from the moaning, bitter winds of winter. Never a hedge to be seen! This is where stonewall country begins and it continues to the borders of Staffordshire, where the limestone walling replaces the gritstone as we pass into Derbyshire.

By now the bus, trundling along the twisting road, passes Whiston Eaves, home of the Squires of Whiston and the gnarled oaks leading to Dusty Stile. And from there, on into Whiston village itself.

Before coming to a halt in Brookhollow, where the Oakamoor Road meets with Black Lane and the main road south to Froghall towards the Potteries and north into the Moorlands and Leek, there was a chance to survey this strung-out village. The road from Froghall wound its way steeply past the chapel, church, village school and scattered cottages with houses in Ross Road, where I was born, leading down into the deep valley edged with red brick cottages with their immaculate gardens; the Sneyd Arms public house, its name reflecting the influence in the area of one of Staffordshire's greatest families; cottages of sandstone and the most dominant building in Brookhollow, the Dovecote, built at the end of the 19th century as a house and village shop which has a dovecote surmounting a tower at the rear of the building.

For me here was journey's end, as the bus shuddered to a halt, by the

The imposing "Dovecote " shop and farm at Brookhollow, Whiston which has little over the years

shop and the distinctive pillarbox-red telephone kiosk (as they used to be called). Up I would jump and with a 'thank you' to the conductor, leap down the step in my eagerness to begin my day out.

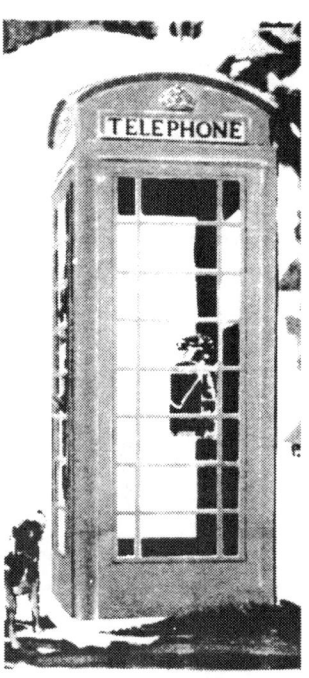

Getting off the bus here by the village shop meant that I could, if I had a few 'coppers' in my pocket to spare, call in the shop to buy two ounces of sweets to eat on the final trek up the hill.

Life, however, is never quite as simple as that, is it? Whiston held a few hazards for a young lad and one of them lay outside the door of the village shop! Often guarding the heavy, studded door to the shop was an enormous (or so it seemed at the time) boxer dog, lying full length, looking very miserable and hungry and likely to savage any person less than five feet tall who might happen to step over him to gain entrance to the shop. As I wished to live another day, and the boxer had no intention of moving, I decided not to risk crossing the threshold when he was there. Mr & Mrs Wordley kept this substantial shop for many years - you will hear more of them and the shop later in the story.

Quickly passing a row of stone cottages situated opposite the shop, I would turn sharply right and up a steep incline known now as Black Lane. I would run as fast as possible up to the first bend in the lane to watch the bus continue its journey onward towards Leek. Round the first corner lived Mr & Miss Keene in a stone cottage, Ivy Cottage to be exact, which was set back from the road. Next to the house were stone buildings and a large barn-type workshop. Outside this building were all sorts of interesting cart wheels and stacks of wood. Looking back across the valley I now had a good view of my old school which I had missed so much when I first moved to Cheadle.

Further up the lane on the opposite side was a solitary, cold looking, farmhouse with a farmyard and outbuildings at its rear. It was known as Stablehouse Farm. The whole of the farmhouse and its buildings were built out of large blocks of waste slag, a bye product of the copper and brass industry and used extensively in the Cheadle district for building walls - but few houses. The blue-black blocks had been faced with plaster on the house itself which made it look not so grim as the rest of the buildings. The blocks were very heavy to move, I once chipped a piece off one and it was like glass inside. I was fascinated by it!

It was at the Stablehouse that I met the next problem which prevented me from proceeding further up the hill - more dogs! The dogs at Stablehouse were more intimidating than the boxer dog below at the shop! They would see you coming from a long way off and would move further into the lane to bar your way.

Today it seems hard to imagine this problem as there are bungalows and houses lining both sides of the lane, but then it was an open grass verge and stone walls all the way up. Slowing down, then listening to the grasshoppers and trying to

Stable House Farm

actually see them in the grass, while wondering how to resolve this dilemma. Getting closer to the dogs all the time. Dare I risk a bite?

The trick was to get close enough for the dogs to make an awful racket without getting close enough to bite - they would only come so far down the lane towards me as, I suppose because they were just protecting their own patch. With luck then, all the barking would bring Mrs Richardson to the side door of Stablehouse to see what the commotion was all about. Whilst she was shouting at them, I could slip past and keep running until I had passed a row of brick-built cottages on the opposite side of the lane - which have since been demolished.

I never did get bitten by these dogs, but it was always best to be safe than sorry! With relief I continued to the top of the bank and passed more buildings which bordered the lane - part of the Top Shop complex of buildings, also now demolished, leaving the shop building looking isolated. The shop was another interesting and substantial building owned by Stoniers. Opposite Stonier's Shop was the entrance to the Common and Whiston Hall, and a heathland of heather, coarse grass and stone, leading to green fields beyond. Then more stone houses and rows of cottages, East View, North

East View, North View, Willow and Stone Cottages

View, Willow and Stone cottages, Finney's Row and another village pub named oddly The Ship Inn. You can't get much further from the sea than Whiston so I have often wondered how it got its name.

Opposite the Ship was a track made of broken blue/black slag by the side wall of Whiston Hall and under the tall trees in which the rooks had their many homes. This track led up to Hall Farm built behind the Hall and owned by Mr Tom Cooper. It also led to a bottomless pit filled

The Ship Inn demolished about 1964

with water which had once provided water for the copper works through an underground passageway.

This track also led to my destination, the home of Mrs Harriet Finney and her daughter Dorothy - number 5, The Plain, Whiston.

31

A rear view of 5, The Plain taken from Whiston Hall Farm track. The new kitchen block was built onto the end of the house where the pig styes once stood.

The view from Whiston School towards Brookhollow

CHAPTER 6
5, The Plain, Whiston

Halfway up the track leading to Hall Farm, opposite the blackened outer wall to Whiston Hall, was the path leading to a stone-built semi-detached house, known as 5, The Plain, which overlooked its own garden and field and with a large field at the rear. A green painted wicket gate barred the entrance to the path, but this was easily opened which usually immediately brought Dorothy's dog Toby to investigate the intrusion.

Walking up the path, on one side was the Cornfield and on the other the Orchard, home to the many hens kept by Dorothy - they peered at you from their temporary perches on the high stone walls. Quickly then, up to the front door, always in those days painted green with a highly polished 5 and a large brass door knob. On the yard in front of both houses was a very large wooden water butt, such as I have never seen since; I could not see into it without pulling myself up to peer over the edge - and this was considered a dangerous thing to do. It was like an enormous wine vat. It was very useful especially in summer for the garden - don't forget there was no mains water laid on then, every drop of drinking water had to be fetched from the well situated in the back field, using two large pails.

The whole area in front of the houses was paved in Staffordshire blue brick, which was scrubbed with Jeyes Fluid to keep it free from slime. Each house was faced with a low garden wall and built into this wall was a washing stillage. From here you could survey the large gardens full of vegetables, strawberries, a large rhubarb patch and nearer the house a flower garden, with roses and cottage garden plants which could survive the Moorland winter winds and late frosts. The washing stillage, originally used for washing yourself, was no longer used by the two ladies, instead it was home to a large, stone head of a classical woman which was a real work of art (as a boy I thought it was a model of Mrs Finney's head!). Sadly this had to be removed years later as it was too valuable to leave outside.

Either side of the classical head were enormous seashells which must have come from faraway seas. They were pure white on the outside, with mother of pearl on the inside. When you held one to your ear you could hear the roar of the sea, from whence they had come - or so I was led to believe. I often wondered at those shells, and where they had come from. I had never been to the seaside at that time so I could only sit and imagine - which I was good at.

From this rather plain, solid, stone-built house which had braved the wind, rain, snow and sun since 1804, the rewas a breathtaking view over the village and for many, many miles beyond. Small farms bounded by sandstone walls; stark tall trees, sheep and cows; all braving the seasonal weather of the Moorlands which could sometimes make Whiston a harsh place to live. No wonder that the stone walls of 5, The Plain were so thick and solidly built to withstand the winter batterings.

The house was really 3 storeys as the ground fell away at the rear so that the cellars were open to the back field. There were a number of outbuildings attached to the house including pig stys, now used as a roosting place for hens, an out-house for young stock, an old workshed and an outside lavatory.

The large back field contained an old orchard with both apple and damson trees. By the well was a single pear tree which fruited only once to my memory. The brick built well provided all the drinking water and the overflow provided a small pond for the solitary duck which Dorothy kept. The ground rose sharply to the high back wall which was the property boundary. In the left hand corner under the steep incline of the old railway was a compound overgrown with trees, where I was to find old bottles and clay pipes in later years. It must have been a Victorian rubbish dump. Over this land roamed many truly free range hens who produced the tastiest eggs you could ever eat - more about hens and eggs later.

Next door to Dorothy lived Lizzie and Jack Ratcliffe, a sister and brother who seemed to me very ancient - at least as old as the house itself! Going past their house it was possible to climb a number of steps up to another green wicket gate which led to the Plain, the steep incline of the tramway which once carried limestone from the Cauldon Low quarries, situated further up into the Moorlands north of Whiston, down to the canal and railway at Froghall and where earlier this century there were large lime kilns.

These houses had a right of way both up and down the incline from where it was possible to get onto Black Lane by the bridge, through a stile.

So now you have an idea of the outside of 5, The Plain, home of Dorothy and her Mother. This house was the base for all my stories. I would like to take you inside the house as it was then, so please join me and enter through that green door with the big brass door knob. But be careful because the door sticks sometimes and makes a scraping sound as it opens.

Come on. Come on in!

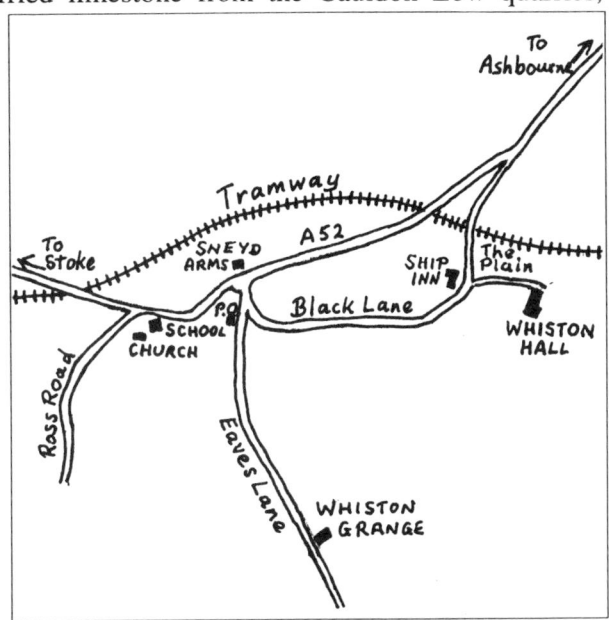

The route of the early tramway along the 'plain'

Lime kilns at Froghall at the end of the tramway

35

The living room at 5 The Plain

CHAPTER 7
"Come on in!"

Toby, Dorothy's black and white collie-cross dog, made an enormous fuss upon your arrival. He would guard the house from a comfortable soft bed of white rock plant , which grew over the flat top of the wall over the pig stys. Toby would bound up to you in a menacing way, barking loudly, until he had found out by sniffing you all over that you were a friend. He would then be all fuss!

Knocking on the door sometimes brought Dorothy to open it, but often Mrs Finney would shout down 'Come on! Come on in!' and I would push open the door, finding myself in a dark hall.

Steep stairs rose straight up in front of you, up to the two bedrooms, one on each side of the stairway. Turning left through a latch door took you into the living room. Turning right took you into the best or front room (these were later changed around when the house was remodelled and a new kitchen and bathroom built onto the end of the house). A smell of polish would pervade your nostrils - the smell of the house which never in all the years seemed to change.

The living room had a very pleasant atmosphere which you felt as soon as you went through the door. A welcoming roaring fire would be burning in the 'modern' range grate, shiny black, spotlessly clean, very different from the old Victorian range next door at the Ratcliffes' house. The range included a water tank, which used to give hot water through a silver tap next to the oven. It had a top oven, used to dry sticks to kindle the fire with and to heat the bedstones (I will tell you of these later!). It also had a large oven in which Dorothy would bake her delicious cakes.

The floor was of red and black tiles covered in places with hand made pegged rugs which were fun to make. This kitchen floor was scrubbed each afternoon, using soft soap from a yellow tin, piping hot water and an old fashioned scrubbing brush. Hard work? Yes. But it looked clean and smelled so fresh!

By the side of the range near the window was a tall built-in cupboard which was an ideal place to keep dry goods, tea towels, Energen rolls, anything in fact which had to be kept dry. This included Penguin chocolate biscuit bars, which I received occasionally as a treat!

Mrs Finney ate 'Energen' rolls

I mentioned Energen rolls, which Mrs Finney ate along with pearl-barley tea, beef tea and Complan - strange food it seemed to me. I once ate an Energen roll which was an unusual experience - one I never repeated - but I did enjoy the 'Dutch Toast' which she also ate. I must admit I felt rather sorry for her having to each such a diet!

Under the window with its deep window sills sat a chaise, on which Mrs Finney would recline in the afternoon - they called it 'the couch'. This couch was a good one covered in leather. It was very old and very comfortable, although I could feel the springs sticking up in odd places!

In the centre of the room was a well-scrubbed

The best 'plush' couch.

pine drop-leaf table which had a handy cutlery drawer at one end. Under this table was Toby's corner, into which he would retreat to sulk when he had been naughty. "Corner!" Dorothy would shout in her no nonsense voice which meant you did as you were told.

On the wall opposite the range, was a large early Victorian sideboard which was full of very unusual Staffordshire jugs with dogs for handles in a blue/green glaze; fascinating they were. There were flat back figurines and old photographs in silver frames. In the drawers were all sorts of treasures, which sometimes came out to illustrate one of the stories for which Mrs Finney was famous. There was the best cutlery, only used for very, very special occasions and in the cupboards were the china tea sets, my favourite having small scattered roses on it.

On the back wall was a small window, which was very useful as it was possible to view the entire back field - nothing was missed from this window - I suppose Dorothy could keep an eye on me from this window when I went on my own adventures roaming the far corners of the field - in a world of my own.

By the side of the range was a comfortable arm chair, into which Dorothy could sink when her daily toil was over. Other times it was occupied by the grey cat, named Toosey, which wasn't the least bit friendly to anyone and was very wild, but a good mouser or even ratter!

Next to the sideboard was a doorway which led down steep brick steps into the cold, dark cellars which housed the coal, the corn stores, the wash house and food stores - not a place to venture on a dark night, except that there was also a collection of unusual walking sticks down there which could have been useful if anyone was lurking down there (as my imagination always thought there was!). The house needed good fires as cold, icy draughts seemed to come from everywhere; doors, windows, floors, but especially from the cellars; a whining noise could always be heard as the wind whistled from the cold dark depths of the house under the cellar door and into the living rooms.

The range gave out a cheery warmth, at least to your front, if not your back. It was all a part of living in Whiston, part of the adventure - at least I tell myself so now!

In my early days all the cooking was done over the range fire, or using the range ovens. Blackened saucepans bubbled and steamed away, hissing occasionally as the boiling water jumped into the red hot coals and steam disappeared up into the chimney. Food made in this way often had a scorched taste, not always unpleasant, giving it a unique country flavour and eaten with relish after a morning in the fresh Whiston air. All the baking preparation was done on the table.

" spotted dick "

"Spotted dick", one of Dorothy's cooking treats

Dorothy made wonderful cakes including seed cake, 'cut and come again fruit cake', tasty scones, Madeira cake, and soft sponge cakes, bright yellow, made with those free range eggs with orange yolks.

All the rugs were taken up every day and beaten with a Victorian carpet beater. This was a job I could be trusted to do - it got rid of lots of energy and a little dust!

I have mentioned that the walls of the house were very thick. The window sills in both rooms were full of Geraniums, Busy Lizzies and Polygoniums all in beautiful pots which made a grand display. The front room was rarely used, like many front rooms in Moorlands villages, only for very special occasions, or Sunday tea when it was the Chapel Anniversary celebration, Harvest and Christmas. Otherwise it was kept in a state of perfection, cleaned and polished in readiness for special visits.

The wooden floor was partially carpeted and was icy cold, even when a fire was lit in the grate. All the best furniture and pictures were kept in this room which included the chest of drawers Dorothy's granny, Sarah Ann, had bought with her from Oulton when she wed Hedley Finney. Dorothy's piano stood on one wall, although this eventually disappeared - I know not where.

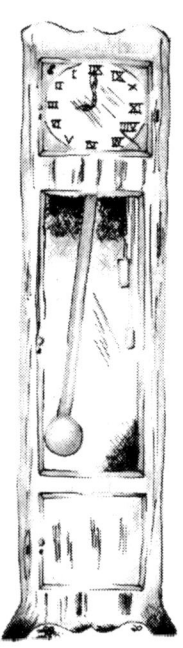

There was also an ancient grandfather clock which had a 'Sun and Moon' movement; the moon had a friendly smiling face I remember. On the chest of drawers, in immaculate condition, stood two fascinating Staffordshire flat back figures which I really loved, one being a sand seller - spelled 'SANB' - which featured an early Victorian male figure selling sand from panniers carried by a mule.

The other was titled 'BEESUMS' which had a young woman with a similar mule, selling old fashioned brushes. I presume these hawkers were a common site in those times. In the middle of the two was an exquisite small writing box in walnut and inlaid mother of pearl.

There was a comfortable 'sofa' and a plush chaise in a dark red wine colour - very smart indeed! The walls were covered in pictures, a needlepoint tapestry, old sepia photographs and over the fireplace a hand-painted mirror.

Upstairs. A steep staircase with a carpet held in place with solid brass rods which looked very stylish, but a pain to clean! On the top wall was a real old hunting horn, a real horn with a silver mouthpiece and chased silver working. I always imagined it was one used by Robin Hood, especially after I was told that Sherwood Forest once stretched into Staffordshire and that there was an old oak tree at nearby Ipstones village which dated back to that time. (Robin Hood and Davy Crockett were my heroes).

To the left was Mrs Finney's bedroom in which she spent a great deal of her time. It was in this bedroom that I would sit - in the deep window sill or on a spindly Georgian chair and listen to her telling stories, in her own warm, distinctive voice. She always had a warm welcome and had an eagerness to hear of all my doings and all about my own family. Although she often repeated the same recollections from her own childhood and all her mishaps at the Squire's home at Whiston Eaves, it was always a pleasure to hear them again and again.

To me then, Mrs Finney - and it wasn't until later years that I would call her Aunty Harriet - was like a rather sedate grandmother sitting up in her bed with very comfortable pillows on which to recline.

She had a large Victorian bed covered with a beautiful hand-embroidered eiderdown in silk, filled with finest eider feathers - very regal it was too! Over the bed was a framed print which said 'Home Sweet Home' and another picture of 'Faith Hope and Charity', wistful ladies in classical attire in some far eastern setting. A small table at the side of the bed was covered in a finely made damask cover on which sat a small travel clock from the days of coach travel and a small brass bell, which she would ring to summon Dorothy from the house below.

On the other side of the bed was a late Georgian washstand in mahogany, with a black and grey marble top. On this stood a large intricately decorated jug and bowl set, which she used each day for her wash. Next to the jug and bowl were her silver hair brushes and hand mirror. Nearby was the large family bible, which occasionally we would open - reading the generations of her family before, looking at the wonderful colour prints which brought the bible stories vividly to life.

From her bed she was able to look out over the top end of the village and its fields - a most pleasant panorama I must say. Climbing into the deep window sill meant I could stare for a long, long time over the beautiful unique countryside, its irregular fields edged in sandstone, the chimneys of Mr. Hambleton's home just over the hillside, Whiston and miles beyond, to

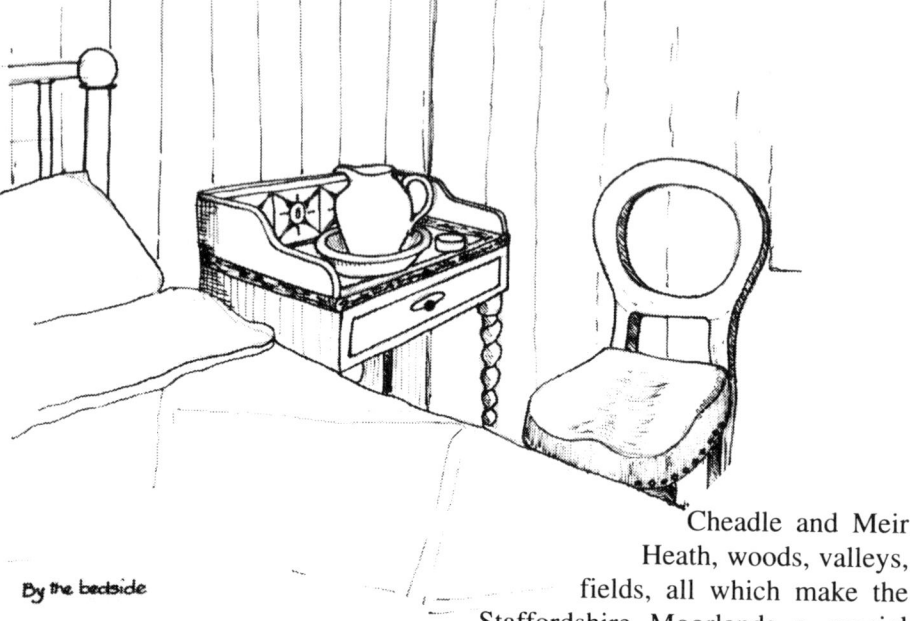

By the bedside

Cheadle and Meir Heath, woods, valleys, fields, all which make the Staffordshire Moorlands a special place in which to live. I soaked it all, the memory was imprinted in my mind like a colour photograph.

In the far corner of the room was a small dressing table which held all sorts of fine china, including a pastille burner in the shape of a house. We once tried it out and smoke came out through the chimneys! There were small Worcester vases bought at the famous Alton Towers sale in the 1920s - these were very special indeed as they were part of the story she told of the great auction. We would stare in wonder at the large sale catalogue. She was very proud to own vases once owned by an Earl. She would tell me the story of King Edward VII being refused entry to Alton Towers by the Countess of Shrewsbury because he had his mistress with him instead of Queen Alexandra! I can't remember if I knew what a mistress was in those young innocent days!

On this far wall was my very favourite picture, which had been a wedding present from her cousin Billy who was a gentleman's gentleman at Fradswell Hall, near the county town of Stafford. It was of an Harbour entwined with roses, with a path leading into the distance to blue sea and hills, a blue sky with white fluffy clouds. I often wished I could walk into this picture and down to the sea which I had never had the pleasure of seeing for myself in real life. This picture now hangs in my own dining room and always brings back those old memories of my childhood. She must have realised how much I loved it as it was left to me when she died.

One of the most frequent stories which Mrs Finney related to me was of a murder in Whiston, at Whiston Eaves, the home of the Squire of the village and his family.

When I was young, Mrs Finney seemed so very ancient herself, I

The Plain

always imagined that the murder happened whilst she was a maid working at the Manor House for this same family! The dastardly deed actually happened in July 1866, when the Squire's bachelor son aged 24 years was shot by his tenant William Collier, when Collier was caught poaching.

Collier tried to shift the blame for the murder onto Gypsies who had been encamped near to Whiston Eaves, until the murder weapon was found in one of Collier's field drains. He was arrested, tried and eventually hanged outside Stafford gaol in August 1866, watched by over 2000 people.

I suppose I wasn't too far away from the truth as Harriet did work at Whiston Eaves for the murdered man's brother, namely John Eli Smith who lived from 1856 to 1929. A full account of this murder can be found in 'Welcome to Whiston' by Joan Morris and the Whiston School Children, published in 1993.

Mrs Harriet Finney was often ill, or too weak to get out of bed for years following her rheumatic fever, which she may have had twice, and then her cancer. She had to be 'careful', only venturing downstairs when the cold room had been well aired in the afternoon. She could not get out to the village, so Whiston came to her, a steady stream of visitors - Mrs Kent, Mrs Beardmore, Lizzie from next door, Lionel Richardson, to mention just a few.

She was kept very well informed about all that was happening in the village - and beyond. She never missed anything! "Come on in!" she shouted to greet your arrival, her smile radiating the warmth of genuine pleasure at your visit. As well as telling stories about the Whiston Eaves murder and its connection with Mary Queen of Scots, of the times of the Civil War when Oliver Cromwell visited the district, of the Shrewsbury Sale at Alton Towers and of her young life in the Moorlands, she would also bring out a large box of games.

As you might imagine these were very old games. They included Happy Families; Snap; Donkey; draughts played on a red and black board; a Victorian Snakes and Ladders and a game called 'Green Label' which involved making the name 'Green Label' by picking cards from a pile - it must have been given away free by a tea company years ago! There was also a similar card game called 'Cow and Gate'. Then there was Lexicon and Solitaire. On wet days the box came out and the hours quickly passed by until it was fit again to go out and roam on the common or pester the hens on the back field!

The whole house was a step back in time and an adventure to be enjoyed. It was cold, yes - and draughty; there were few of the conveniences we now take so much for granted. But nothing can replace those idyllic times in Whiston - what memories!

Harriet Finney on her 90th
birthday

Harriet and Dorothy share
a joke at Christmas 1984

The great slab of stone on the 'Common' and below, the Back field

CHAPTER 8
Mr Hambleton and the Wheelbarrow

Next to the garden was what seemed to me to be a large meadow field - although it now seems much smaller. It belonged to Mrs Finney and was known as the Cornfield. The hens, always looking for worms and any creepy-crawlies, would fly over from the orchard into it, to scratch around the hedge at the top of this field. They would sometimes hollow out dust baths here for themselves in summer, but in the main they tended to stay on the back field.

I once startled a fox having a nap under the hedge. I don't know who was the most startled him or me, but we both fled in opposite directions!

In the middle of this field was a marvellous tree, I say marvellous because it had low branches which made it easy to climb. I never had a head for heights and I had two left feet and although often called "you young monkey!", climbing trees did not come naturally to me. This tree, however, I could manage - up, up, up into the high branches and I sat watching the world go by in my leafy surroundings; watching life in Whiston go by - very slowly! From up in the boughs of the tree I could see over the blackened curtain wall of the Old Hall and watch the rooks in their trees, wheeling, cawing, turning, returning dutifully to their large nests which were full of young birds beginning their new young lives, swelling the noise it seemed, a hundredfold.

Once a year, in late summer, the field would be mowed, the grass dried in the sun and made into hay which was then carried away by tractor and trailer. The corners and edges of the irregular shaped field were then cut, using the large scythes which were kept in the old shed next to the pig stys. Hanging on the wall in the gloomy darkness of the shed were a selection of scythes, some taller than me and considered very dangerous because of their sharp blades. I was forbidden to go near them and warned not to touch them. There were also two smaller hand scythes which they called 'badging hooks'.

Mr. Hambleton once decided to give me a demonstration. He told me stories of the old days of harvesting long ago. A dozen men, as brown as berries with working their entire lives exposed to the elements, would take up their scythe blades to sharpen them, using hand stones which were up to a foot long, which they flicked from side to side with great speed and accuracy along the long curved blades. They would often wear a hat to protect their

heads from the hot, summer sun; they wore shirts with no collars and corduroy trousers which were hardwearing. These trousers came up to their armpits with braces holding them up, or with a thick leather belt fastened round their middles. The trousers were gartered with strips of leather or sometimes dried eel skins which were supposed to ward off rheumatism and keep away the ague which was considered a village curse. They also stopped mice running up their trouser legs causing comic contortions (and possible disaster!).

The men would, when in the fields, swing their scythes in a graceful motion with their blades cutting effortlessly, an acre per man per day. The harvest was carried into the farm on a large dray pulled by an enormous Shire horse, who was fitted out with a straw hat for the occasion, his ears sticking through holes made in the straw - a scene of rural majesty with a good sense of humour!

When the harvest was over, an enormous Harvest Supper would be held in the farmhouse, the groaning tables full of every good food the farmers wife could provide. This was a men only occasion and one which could lead to thick heads the following morning. The fare was roast beef, Yorkshire

Pudding, roast fowl, enormous apple pie with fresh cream, plum duff and Derbyshire mature cheese. Local strong beer and cider flowed from pewter pint pots into men thankful that the harvest was in for another year.

Mr Hambleton decided to give me a demonstration in the dying art of scything. Carefully taking down the scythe from its bracket on the wall, he took out his sharpening stone and started to sharpen the rusting blade very rapidly - until it was indeed lethal in its sharpness. He looked it up and down then jokingly handed it over to me but I stepped back, wondering what Dorothy would say if she could see me!

"Thee dustna know how fut use it dust thee lad?" he joked. "Come thee on an' arl show thee," he said taking the scythe with him walking towards the field with his usual gait and his cloth cap pushed backwards on his head at a jaunty angle.

It was obvious that he had used this kind of implement many times before. Once in the Cornfield he measured his stroke.

"Keep thee well back, wootna? Ar dunna want fut tak thee legs off," he growled. I looked at the blade and moved quickly out of the way, I didn't want to lose my legs either yet! He gave the blade a final swish up and down for its final honing, then began his scything in a graceful sweeping motion, the grass falling rapidly before him. I imagined teams of such countrymen in the fields moving hay, corn or wheat in the same way Mr Hambleton was doing before my own eyes.

He told me that local country lengthsmen had kept the grass verges throughout the county well trimmed using the same method. It was good to watch this old countryman, who was so practical, being able to turn his hand to anything, with his collarless shirt sleeves rolled up and his trousers up under his armpits, held up with braces and tied under the knee in case of mice! His face was rugged, bronzed by the sun and wind. He was a character who stuck proudly to his Moorlands dialect. "Dunt they teach thee ote at skool?" he would chide, with a grin when I struggled to help carry out a simple task which I found so hard but he found so easy.

When digging out a trench in the back field, he unearthed several old bottles. It was an exciting find indeed - ancient bottles, wow! Beer bottles, lemonade bottles, etc, in green glass and brown glass stamped with the brewery name and with glass marbles in their necks to control the flow of liquid. He smashed one of the bottles and pulled out the glass marble and put it on the palm of his hand. It was fascinating to think that this piece of treasure which had been buried for so many years was now rediscovered. I wondered who had drunk from the bottle and then discarded it! He held it up to the light - a greenish blue glass ball filled with minute air bubbles.

To me it seemed priceless. "Put it in thee pocket," said Mr Hambleton grinning, then he proceeded to smash others, each time removing the marbles, all different and equally fascinating. Looking back now, I rather wish that I had kept the bottles whole with their local brewery names, long since gone. Ah well, that often happens in life, doesn't it?

My daughter now has a collection of these bottle herself and looking at them brings back memories of the unearthed treasure from the trench dug by Mr Hambleton all those years ago.

Back in the old outbuilding where the scythes were kept, were also a multitude of other implements and odds and ends which would now grace any country-life museum. In one corner was a very large, very heavy, wooden wheelbarrow. This wheelbarrow was brought out for gardening purposes. Thinking back, it looked just like the one in Beatrix Potter's Mr McGregor's garden.

When Dorothy was weeding her large garden, the wheelbarrow was sent for. It was very hard to manoeuvre out of the building, then wobbling from side to side it was pushed up the incline in front of the house and through the gate and down the garden path to where shewas working. Once it was full, the barrow was backed up the path, then turned around, back down the track to the back field, which was fairly steep for a heavy

50

wheelbarrow to be controlled. The idea was to empty the contents for the hens to scratch through in search of earthworms, wireworms and other creatures along with the tasty green leaves. Unfortunately, going much too fast around the corner and down the incline the barrow came to a shuddering halt as the wheel flew off, scattering the waiting hens in a mass of feathers, flying bodies and screeching. The barrow that was being pushed so fast, came to a sudden halt, but I didn't - I went head over heels, over the barrow - and into the mud!

Naturally, I got the blame for the whole episode. I had been going too fast. This had caused too much strain on the spindle which held the wheel in place - it was used to being pushed sedately and the shock of my reckless driving had given it a nervous breakdown!
Mr Hambleton, I understand, made a new spindle for the wheel and the old wheelbarrow lived on for a few more years. I had learned my lesson and in future pushed it in the way it liked and not like "Stirling Moss".

Dorothy's Jack Russell, Romp, and myself
on the wall of the cornfield

51

CHAPTER 9
The Good, the Bad and the Downright peevish!

So what was so attractive about a way of life which was certainly not easy? Indeed, there was no piped running water, no electric cooker, no television until later years, no central heating, no washing machine and poor sanitation. Going to the 'lavatory' was something done only when absolutely necessary - the lavatory was a brick building situated at the back of the house a short distance from the rear entrance to the cellars and within view of the cellar window.

As you would imagine it was a functional building with a brick floor and a single scrubbed pine seat situated over a pan, which was collected and emptied each week by the 'Lavatory Men' who had quite a number of such collections in the Whiston area, including the village school. I was always told to keep out of the way when they were around. At the school when I was very young we would taunt them with shouts of "Pooh!" and "Stinkers!" in response to which they would chase us around the playground. If any poor creature was caught they would have smelly hands rubbed around their faces - all in good fun but hardly hygienic. Naturally the day before collection the smell from the pan was at its worst, especially in summer, even though Dorothy would liberally sprinkle a white sanitary powder all over the 'night soil' as it was called. This is where I first learned to hold my breath for as long as possible. Alas, never long enough which resulted in almost heaving because of the awful smell. This was one part of the old way of life which I was pleased to see pass into history!

I have mentioned also a few times already that Dorothy kept a huge flock of hens or 'fowl' as she called them. Many of them were Rhode Island Reds with some pure white ones and an old fashioned speckledy variety. She also kept bantams too on occasions. There must have been 50 to 60 at any one time. They were watched over by two giant cockerels who were particularly mean looking, for all their colourful plumage.

Hens, as anyone who has anything to do with them knows, are particularly peevish to both humans and their own kind and their jabbing beaks can feel quite sharp. They are quite stupid and unpredictable especially to someone who was 'afeared' of them. Hens are always hungry and always hanging around waiting for their food at feeding time - or any other time for that matter - in fact everytime I emerged through the cellar door where they knew the corn and meal was kept. Pushing through them to get to the lavatory I would throw a handful of corn as far away as possible which meant they would all leave the way clear, squabbling, jabbing, squarking whilst they scrambled for the food. It was always a mistake to do this since seconds later, looking for more food, they would barricade the lavatory door, lying in wait for when I emerged. No matter how long I waited, they still waited, longer congregating in a mass of feathers, beaks and the two very ferocious cocks. The only thing you could do in that situation was make a run for it - scattering hens everywhere with loud squarking noises, as if they were being murdered, silly creatures! This was in the days when boys wore short trousers which meant that jabbing beaks at your legs made it a painful experience! Strange isn't it, what worries you at that age? But there again, YOU try having a host of 'fowl' pecking at you!

As you have seen, hens and I did not always trust each other! Perhaps worse than the ordeal of going to the lavatory was egg collecting - what could be the problem with this I hear you asking? Well, in the main it was good fun, most of the nesting boxes were easy to get at and it was easy to tell when a hen had finished laying her egg because of the noise she made.

However, some of the wretched creatures would lay their eggs in the old pig sty. It was very, very dark inside the sty, it had a very low entrance, so even at my age I had to crouch down to get inside. If the 'flashlight' wasn't working - and often the battery was so low there was no more than a glimmer - "drat!" Feeling for the nesting box and praying there was no fowl there - where is it? Was there a feathery creature lying in wait? Occasionally the prayer was answered and my hand would feel straw and a clutch of eggs - and a feeling of relief. But often my hand would come down on a very quiet hen, making no noise whatsoever, until that is my hand came out of the darkness onto a feather ball. Surely it had seen me come in through the low entrance?

The Pig sty

Up would fly the indignant creature into your face screeching loudly as if it was having its throat cut!

Jumping backwards in horror I would stand up straight, banging my head on the rafters, then dive outside following the hen as if 'Owd Nick' himself was after me.

There again, it was worth it just to taste a 'Dorothy egg'. Imagine - truly free range, fed on the best corn and with a totally unstressed life - except of their own making of course. Oh! and of course the possibility of one day ending in the pot when their egg laying days were well and truly over! Yes, to dip a crusty 'soldier' covered in butter into a boiled 'Dorothy egg' was memorable indeed. Definitely worth the odd headache caused by a savage fowl!

After the eggs were collected they had to be washed in hot semi-soapy water, using a scrubbing brush and very carefully - not too heavy handed. Take out the 'double yolkers' and any which might be soft shelled - if they survived. The rest were dried and placed in large cardboard egg trays which held 24 brown speckled eggs each. All ready for the 'Eggman' to call.

The Eggman was from the Egg Marketing Board and the eggs would, after collection and processing, be stamped with a little lion which was supposed to be a mark of quality but often meant they were old by the time they reached the shops.! Whoever was fortunate enough to buy Dorothy eggs had a treat, I can tell you.

The double-yolked eggs were put into a bowl ready for baking day, as were any soft shelled eggs which hadn't had a finger poked in them by some young 'varmant'! Eggs were also supplied to the villagers - those who didn't have their own supply. They were carefully wrapped in strips of newspaper ready for collection. Fowls which got too old for egg laying were sold off in the village. Sometimes I would take one home but that's another story!

CHAPTER 10
Waking up in Whiston

In the summer holidays, which were six weeks at least and seemed like an eternity, I was allowed to go and stay at Dorothy's for a whole week or more. This meant great excitement and anticipation of the fun filled days to come which would be enjoyable whether it rained or not.

Arriving on the bus in Whiston with a small bag of summer clothes, a large box of Kelloggs 'Frosties' and a toothbrush, Dorothy would meet me and take me back to the house - me talking non-stop about things I would like to do during my prolonged stay.

I was allowed to take over Dorothy's bedroom, whilst she was banished to a bed made up on the couch downstairs. This was very kind of her, but she said she didn't mind at all.

Dorothy was always used to getting up at the crack of dawn and I was determined to be up early myself, so that not a minute was wasted. And that's

what happened. Soon after the cock's crowing began, jumping out of bed, so cold even in summer - the heat of the day never seemed to penetrate the thick stone walls. After a cool night the air in the bedroom seemed icy. Throwing back the curtains, looking out over a still sleeping village, although wisps of smoke were already coming from some of the nearby farms, who always seemed to be awake at this time of day, doing half a days work before breakfast. Breakfast? Yes, my stomach told me it was empty, but it would have to wait until later as you will see.

The old house always seemed friendly even at the dead of night when it creaked and groaned in the winds which often blow over the top of the hill, whistling around the house in a battle to take off the roof. Sometimes slates would come crashing down, but it was a house built to last and it always felt secure even in the worst weather. Opening the bedroom window, breathing in the morning air - sometimes warmer outside than in - the sky seemed full of birdsong, not so loud as in springtime but pleasant and contrasting with the incessant cawing of the nearby rookery in the Whiston Hall grounds. The noise mixed with the crowing of the cockerels and the squarking of the hens who were already let out of their coops and now awaiting their breakfasts, quarreling amongst themselves in their usual fashion.

Dressed in seconds, carefully lifting up the latch of the bedroom door, which creaked loudly as the door opened, creeping downstairs on tip toe, trying to miss the stairs which made too much noise, I would reach the hallway. Hopefully I hadn't awakened Mrs Finney. Into the living room, warmer than upstairs, but no fire in the range yet. The room smelled inviting, looked very tidy, the breakfast things were laid on the pine table. My stomach grumbled again. No sign of Dorothy though, she must have been up at 5 am to start the days work. It was now nearer to six.

Hearing noises down below in the cellar, I forgot about feeling hungry and decided to go down the cellar steps to see if I could help Dorothy with the morning 'jobs'. There would be no breakfast until then.

Opening the cellar door led onto a pantry before the twenty or so steep brick steps dropped down to the cellar rooms below. The shelves held all the spare eggs for baking, pearl barley, rice, semolina, other dry goods, dried peas, beans, jelly moulds and meat paste moulds, all pretty ancient. This is where the Lucozade was kept, which was only given as a rare treat because of the high price of it.

Behind the door was an old brown overall or 'slop' as it was called. It was rather baggy and came down to my knees, but it was warm and kept you clean - which meant less washing which was always a good thing (both clothes and even more so, myself!).

At the bottom of the steps, a right turn brought you to the first cellar room named the 'Wash-house' (or Wesh Us). It was icy cold in here - never seeing sunshine, with a cold blue brick floor. It was attractive however, because of all the unusual things to be found there - all very neat of course; everything in its place as always. There were the big wash tubs, a dolly peg and paunch clothes tongues for handling boiling washing, along with the clothes horses, all waiting for the Monday washday. An old built-in boiler was next to a charming window which looked out on the back field. Under the window was a shallow brown sink, which filled me with trepidation as it was where I was supposed to have a good wash twice a day (like Queen Elizabeth I - whether I needed it or not!).

In the cellar were rows of jars

Two long shelves, which ran the length of the wall, housed bottles, Kilner jars and jam jars full of picked onions, picked shallots, red cabbage, Dorothy's famous beetroot pickle, green tomato chutney, even damsons (ugh!). Alongside these were jar after jar of strawberry, raspberry, gooseberry, blackcurrant, rhubarb and ginger, blackberry, damson and plum jams, and if this wasn't enough, marmalade - enough to feed a small army I thought.

On the wall opposite was an old tin bath - the thought of having a bath down in that cold cellar sent a shiver down my back, but the bath was taken upstairs in front of the range fire, so perhaps that wasn't too bad. Otherwise I would have preferred to stay dirty! In the corner stood two large, white enamelled pails which were used to fetch all the water needed for house use and were heavily used on Wash day. By the pails was the meat safe, the equivalent of today's fridge. The meat safe was really useful. It was a large cabinet made from wood with wire mesh doors and sides. It allowed cold air to circulate, but kept out flies, bluebottles and squeaking intruders! Dorothy and her mother liked their meat but as there was no butcher in the village, they had to rely on a weekly delivery from a butcher who I think came from Oakamoor.

A delivery was made by a large man who really looked the part - he had a red face. He wore a straw boater, crisp white overall and a blue striped apron. The meat was brought into the house in a very large wicker basket overfilled with meat - enough to last a week. This consisted, usually, of a beef joint for the weekend, an ox-tongue for cooking and pressing before slicing and using on sandwiches, an ox tail for braising, brains for making brawn, black pudding and sausage. Watching Dorothy boiling the long ox tongue, then pressing it, put me off eating tongue for years until I became averse to eating any meat at all. But I have gone off my tale a little - so now back to the cellar!

Before I could start work, I knew I must wash my face and neck at least, so it was best to get it over with quickly. No hot water in the bowl, just ice cold well water and a bar of Wright's Coal Tar Soap. This was followed by vigorous rubbing of soap and water on my face, then rubbing with a soft towel leaving my face, ears and yes, my neck clean and warm!

Smelling of coal tar and still a little damp, it was time to join Dorothy in the other cellar room, which had a door to the outside. One half of this room was full of coal and logs held back by huge blocks of coal which I was told had come from Shaffalong (near Cheddleton) many years before. They were never used but made a good barrier to put lump coal behind.

On the other side of the room were all the supplies needed to feed the army of hens. Two large barrels, much taller than me, held split corn and laying pellets. There was a sack full of maize flakes and another full of bran. Dorothy then, was making a mash for their breakfasts. Bran, Maize and Corn with a teaspoon or two of Carswoods spice (which helped laying). Boiling water was added and all stirred together. It smelled like wet cardboard with a hint of spice - but the hens loved it. To get corn and pellets meant standing on a stool then reaching down inside the barrels, with an empty 'Snowcem' paint tin which was used as a measure. Everything was fine if the corn was near the top of the barrel but if a delivery was expected, the level would be

low down, which meant delving deep down. Need I tell you what happened? Well, reaching down too far, I lost my balance and went head first into the barrel with my feet sticking out of the top.

Luckily Dorothy was at hand to pull me out, but I was covered in dust and corn. My worst nightmare was that there would be a rat or mouse waiting inside one of the barrels, rather like the hen waiting in the pig sty! Toosey, the cat, spent long periods in the cellar and was a good mouser, in fact this grey stripey cat was equally vicious to humans and mice and wasn't an animal to ever sit on your knee purring contentedly.

Dorothy had stirred the hens' breakfast with a large paddle. I too gave it a stirring, then took it outside feeling like the Pied Piper with a huge following of hens all around me, jabbing at the bucket and at my legs! They soon forgot me as soon as the breakfast mash was emptied on the ground for them - all they had to do then was squabble amongst themselves.

Taking the empty bucket back and washing it out ready for the next meal, I then took an old watering can around the various water holders. Next, the nesting boxes were cleaned out and fresh straw added, replacing the pottery dummy eggs which were placed in the nesting box to encourage hens to lay there - hopefully by the late afternoon there would be lots of eggs to collect.

It would soon be time for breakfast, but still there was another job to complete; fresh water had to be fetched from the well in the centre of the back field. The two large white pails in the cellar were used for this. Dorothy could carry two full pails of water at a time, but this was too much for me and I had to make two trips. The well had been modernised and was contained in a brick structure which, when you opened the door, you could dip the bucket into the deep fast-flowing spring which welled up from underground. Like most things at Dorothy's, the water was icy cold - just the thing on a hot summer's day. When I was bigger and could manage two buckets, there was always the danger that the water would slop over the edge of the pail and straight into my wellingtons - not a pleasant sensation at all!

Taking off my wellingtons and slop, it was time to follow Dorothy back upstairs to the living room. This was short lived as I would be ordered back down into the wash house cellar room to once again wash my hands and face - once is enough for one morning, surely, but no, they had to be done again whether they were dirty or not!

By the time I returned, having discovered a collection of old walking sticks in a dark corner to amuse myself, the breakfast was well on its way and a fire was beginning to burn brightly in the range with bangs and crackles of dried sticks burning away under the lumps of coal. After a windy day it was fun to go 'sticking' with Dorothy, taking an old sack and filling it with small sticks and twigs from the old trees across the common. These were kept in the cellar, then dried so many at a time in the range cooker.

Nothing smells better to a hungry lad than the smell of cooking bacon and eggs eaten with large slices of crusty white bread and tomato sauce. This was not an everyday happening as often it would just be a boiled egg or cornflakes. Today was indeed a treat and I enjoyed every last bit - mopping up every bit of 'dip' so that the plate didn't need much washing! It was washed down with large cups of tea. What better way to start a long day in the summer!

Next came the ritual of getting Mrs Finney's breakfast prepared. A large breakfast tray with a lace cloth was laid out. On it was placed a silver toast rack, china butter dish, marmalade in a silver holder, a small individual china tea pot, tiny cream jug, sugar bowl and a plate to eat from. All the height of elegance.

Toast was made by holding a slice of bread on a long brass toasting fork in front of a bright, red fire - not too close or it burned too quickly, when it was golden brown and smelled delicious it was time to do the other side. Dorothy would then cut off all the crusts with a sharp knife - I sometimes ate these as I considered them to be the best bits. The tea was made, placed on the tray and then taken up to Mrs Finney's room above, where she would be propped up in bed, looking a picture awaiting her morning feast! I wasn't allowed to carry the tray upstairs, as it was rather heavy and it would have been unforgivable to have dropped it.

If Dorothy was a little late, the bell by Mrs Finney's bed would tinkle and Dorothy would shout that it was on its way! The bell would tinkle again when the tray, empty of food, was ready to be fetched down. This is when the washing up was done on the living room table. An oil cloth was put over the table, a wooden board was placed on top of it and then an enamelled bowl on top of this. Hot water was drawn from the tank by the range in a large tin jug and poured into the bowl. I would do the washing up and Dorothy would do the drying, for although washing myself was something to be avoided, messing in water could be enjoyable!

Looking at the clock it was only 10 o'clock and it seemed as though a whole day had passed already, even though it had hardly begun. One thing was for sure, the holiday in Whiston was going to be good fun.

CHAPTER 11
Around the Village

After putting away all the breakfast things and when all was ship-shape, it was usual for Dorothy and I to walk down the hill to the village shop in Brookhollow for any provisions which were needed.

I would be sent round to 'Lizzies' next door to see if she needed anything herself; if, that is, I could understand what she said (you will hear more about this lovely 'mouse-like' woman later).

Toby would be left behind to guard the house whilst we were away and off we went down the track, looking up at the rookery by the Hall, then down Black Lane enjoying the view over the hills and valleys to Cheadle and beyond. Down, down the steep bank, past Stablehouse Farm, where the two dogs who waited and barred my path so often when I was on my own were strangely mute and moved silently out  of the way when Dorothy walked past. But there again they knew her well, as she often called in to visit the Richardsons who lived there.

Down at the 'Bottom' shop as it was then called, which was also the Post Office, the boxer dog was in his usual place, but now we could step over him and push open the heavy door with its clangy bell warning those inside someone was coming, without any problem - the boxer never lifted an eyebrow!

Once inside the shop, which smelled absolutely wonderful, the mingling smells of fresh crusty bread, cakes, and other smells associated with a village shop that sold literally everything. Often the smell of cooking dinner would also waft through to the shop from the living quarters behind.

The shop was a family business run at that time by Mr & Mrs Wordley and in later years by a family named Tudor. Mr. Wordley was a tall man, (as all grown-ups are to the younger generation), who always wore a brown overall and a cap, as I don't seem to remember him having much hair! I always felt that he looked very much like his dog especially as his overall was the same colour!

Mrs Wordley was a no-nonsense business woman who I must admit rather frightened me. She had a red complexion and a sharp voice, but no doubt she was very kind really!

While Dorothy did business at the Post Office counter, I would stare at all the shelves stocked with jars of sweets - Old 'Betty Plants' with an old grandmother on the label, 'Halls', Victory V's in a red tin and Uncle Joe's Mint Balls. But most of the sweets were out of my price range. The most expensive were 'buttered brazils' which were 1 shilling and ten pence for a quarter of a pound!

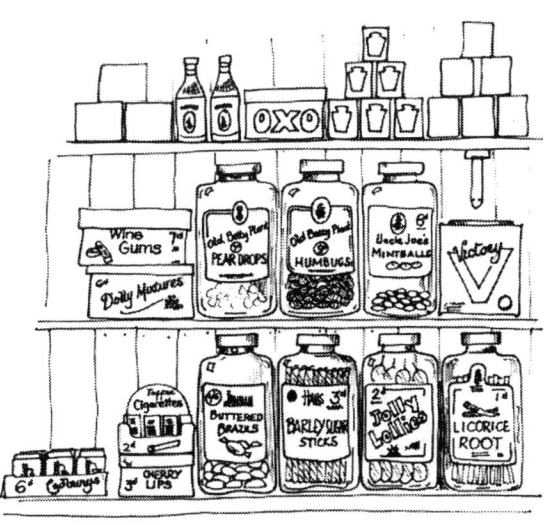

Rows of sweet jars in the village shop

The shop was not only the place to buy stamps and food, it was also the centre for gossip, where all the latest village news was mulled over and discussed. This tended to take a long time! Having studied all the shelves and the large bacon slicer and then the refrigerated display, the last things to examine were the fly papers hanging from the ceiling, covered in black blobs which had once been flies. With all the gossip now exchanged and Dorothy's

bag packed, it was off again, through the
door, over the boxer - who still hadn't
moved - and back up the bank.

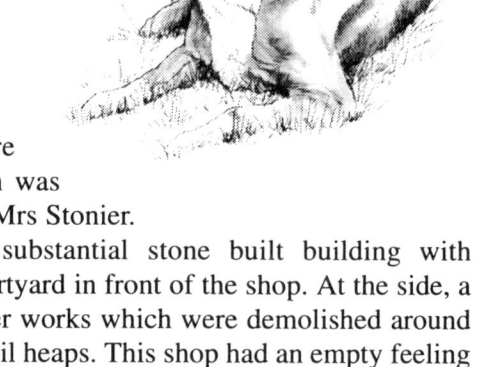

Dorothy would call in at
Miss Keenes, Ivy Cottage to
collect the milk. I never saw
much of her because I was
always left outside to wander up
and down the path! Other calls
were made to Stablehouse and to
cottages now demolished before
calling in to the 'Top' shop, which was
run by a most pleasant lady named Mrs Stonier.

The top shop was another substantial stone built building with
outbuildings facing it, making a courtyard in front of the shop. At the side, a
track led to the site of the old copper works which were demolished around
1910 and the remains of the slag-spoil heaps. This shop had an empty feeling
as though it was very big inside, with a long counter, I can't remember it
having much to sell. What they did sell was the best, most crusty bread you
could ever taste. The whole shop was filled with the smell of this. Dorothy
always bought her bread from Stoniers until the shop closed a few years later.

The large loaves were wrapped in large sheets of tissue paper twisted at
the ends. It stopped you from nibbling the corners off the bread as you
walked back to the Plain (I did this once - Dorothy was not amused). Mrs
Stonier would stand patiently behind her scrubbed pine counter kept very
clean whilst I would pick the sweets I wanted. Mrs Stonier was not only a
jolly lady, but was a relation too on my mother's side of the family. She was
also very generous; she always threw a few extra pear drops into the bag for
good measure. Pear drops were my favourite boiled sweet, sweetly acid
which cut your tongue terribly but worth it! She would ask how my family
was and give a big smile when I handed over my pennies in payment. Yes, I
liked Mrs Stonier and the friendly welcome of the 'top shop'.

On, around the corner, Dorothy would call in at Mrs Beardmore's and
then to Mrs Spencer's who lived at North View, a brick built house with very
little view and oddly built onto the corner of Stone Cottage after the
demolition of the copper works. You will hear more of the Spencers in a later
chapter.

The last place to call was to Willow Cottage where Mrs Finney had spent her first years of marriage to Jack. The Richardsons lived there then with their son Paul and daughter Andrea who also were regular callers at Dorothy's. Mr Richardson was a big help to Dorothy giving good advice whenever she needed it.

Lastly she would shout 'hello' to Mrs Barker who lived in the end cottage before trudging back to 5, The Plain, where time was getting on and thoughts of dinner were in the mind of one growing lad!

The kettle, blackened on the one side which received most of the heat, was on the fire in no time. It had soon bubbled away and the steaming water poured into the large 'Brown Bessie' teapot. Lizzie from next door would be invitied around for a cup and one would be taken up to Mrs Finney along with 'Morning Coffee' biscuits. If I was lucky I would be given a chocolate 'Penguin' bar or even a bar of Frys 'Five Boys' chocolate. Lizzie would chatter away but without her false teeth in, so as usual it was almost  impossible for me to tell what she was saying, but she would grin a big toothless smile and I would smile back and nod, hoping this was a sufficient reply.

With such refreshments out of the way it was time to consider dinner; a simple dinner but always very welcome. The potatoes were peeled with a very sharp knife and would soon be bubbling away on the fire. I was sent down the garden to fetch some fresh mint, which then had to be chopped very finely - add vinegar and sugar - hey presto, mint sauce. So dinner was served, potatoes, peas (which had been soaked overnight) and cold roast ham, thickly cut. This was put onto hot plates, butter and my handmade mint sauce, and devoured with great relish.

It was all washed down with cold fresh water from the well. Occasionally Dorothy would make a tasty 'Spotted Dick' pudding which was boiled in a large pan. The suety pudding studded with currants and sultanas was wrapped in a pudding cloth and boiled for a long time - but the result was a splendid pudding, served with lashings of hot custard. She was also an expert at making treacle pudding and jam roly-poly, a feast fit for a King!

More washing up then it was time for me to go 'out of the way' whilst all the rugs were taken up and the floor scrubbed.

So I would take Toby for a walk across the common and perhaps into my own imaginary world in the back field waging war on the nettles - usually getting stung and having to rub the stung area with a trusty dockleaf.

Soon it was time to feed the hens their split corn and laying pellets and following this to search for eggs, taking the 'flash light' and an old wicker basket in which to place the fresh eggs. Sometimes a hen would decide to lay away somewhere in the back field, especially if it was broody. These eggs had to be found and the hen encouraged back to lay in the nests provided.

As well as having a large number of hens, Dorothy also had one duck. I don't know where it came from but it lived with the hens for a long, long time. This duck was a dirty beige colour and was extremely noisy. How it survived so long I'll never know but it did. It never had a name, it was just called the 'duck'. It had a minute pond to swim around which in reality was the overflow from the well. The duck happily swam round and round, paddling in circles, sometimes quacking quietly for a change to itself. The hens, peevish as usual, would peck at the duck if it came near to them, so it had quite a lonely existence.

Occasionally, the duck would lay an egg which Dorothy would use for baking. I was rather put off duck eggs when Mr Hambleton from the smallholding over the hill, who you've already heard about, came to empty a cess pit, the duck proceeded to lap all that came out of it and in a very greedy fashion as if it was a feast. This was known as 'soc-holling'.

The duck disappeared one day. I was told it died of old age - but I was never sure.

The afternoon soon passed and by the time all the jobs were done and, having washed my hands yet again in the cellar before climbing back up the stairs, I went inside into the living room. The floor nicely dried and the rugs relaid, the room looked spick and span and old Mrs Finney would be sitting on the couch in front of the fire.

Just in time for mid-afternoon tea which was a cup of tea in the best scattered rose-patterned china cups and saucers with scones, spread with butter and raspberry jam. Toby always looked up at me longingly begging for scraps, but it was forbidden to give him any because he was getting too fat. If Dorothy wasn't looking, I would sneak him a bit of scone which he really appreciated. I would fetch the tin from upstairs and we would play draughts and 'Green label'. I think Mrs Finney enjoyed this as much as I did.

The day was wearing on and it was time for tea which was a lettuce from the garden - usually a cos lettuce with long crunchy leaves, a tomato, radishes from the garden with pickled onions and beetroot relish from the cellar wolfed down with more slices of crusty bread spread thickly with butter. More cups of tea in the second best earthenware cups and saucers and slices of Caraway seed cake.

Full to bursting and the washing up done it was time to take Toby across the common for his evening walk and watch the sun beginning to drop down towards the horizon, the hills and valleys turning a blue grey colour in the still summer evening air. Then, feeling rather tired after a momentous day, it was back to Dorothy's to help shut up the fowls for the night and put everything ready for the morning. Forced to have a final wash of the day, which I'm sure I didn't need, it was time for my supper of Frosties, which I had brought with me from Cheadle, washed down with 'Bournvita', alternated every other night with Ovaltine.

There was no argument about going to bed at nine o'clock into the fresh smelling bed, the window left open a crack so I could hear the night creatures about outside. The owls hooting, a vixen calling and lots of other noises I could only guess at. A wonderfully fulfilling time full of good memories. I felt very lucky to be there, in Whiston, enjoying all the country had to offer and enjoying every minute. I always fell asleep immediately for it was soon morning and another full day!

CHAPTER 12
Aunty Louie Visits

A time which I looked forward to and enjoyed each summer at Dorothy's was the annual visitation of one of the nicest ladies I have ever known. Aunty Louie, as she was known, was very much the Edwardian Lady but without any stiffness. She enjoyed having fun, which was fine by me. She would arrive at 5, The Plain for several weeks during August to give Dorothy a break from her life of toil, allowing her to make visits further afield without having to have the constant worry as to whether her mother was safe. Aunty Louie was no spring chicken and I felt sorry for her at times when she struggled with some of the jobs she had to do. She was always pleased when I offered to help.

Aunty Louie was Jack Finney's Cousin from Oulton, near Stone. She, like Harriet, had gone into service and tragically, like many others, lost the love of her life in the 1914-18 Great War and never married, which was a great shame as she had a lovely personality. For most of her working life, until she retired, she lived in Shrewsbury as housekeeper and latterly as a companion. She always returned to the homestead in Oulton as often as she could. She was a warm person with a big smile and a great deal of patience. In all the years I knew her she never had a bad word to say for anyone,

even when she had good cause. I can hear her saying now, "If you can't do anyone a good turn, then never do them a bad one". She wouldn't put up with gossip either. Like Harriet she too had lots of stories to tell, especially about her favourite part of the country which was the Lake District around Keswick. She would pull out her old photographs and although never vain, she was a good looking lady when young. Aunty Louie was also Great Aunt to my future wife, Rosamund and would tell me how she was getting along after we first met at Dorothy's, as you'll hear later. We often visit Shrewsbury ourselves and always think of her, especially in the 'Dingle' which she loved dearly.

She always wore a warm, dark brown dress, or at least that's how I remember her, with a large Victorian brooch which she told me had been her Mothers.

Aunty Louie always loved picnics or any alfresco meal, which as it was summer when she visited, we often had. All the work would be done, then she would prepare a few sandwiches and cakes, an apple and orange with a flask of tea all packed in a wicker basket, and off we went with Toby.

Over the common we would trek, through the fields beyond towards Moneystone. We would stop in our favourite place under the trees, looking down the valley to an old stone barn known as Whiston Barn, standing close by thick woodland and the place where we spread out the cloth. Our array of

food was covered in thousands of daisies which she would make into a daisy chain for her hair! If she could she would walk further into the woodland searching for bilberries, which I remember took a great quantity to make anything with! We would saunter slowly back into Whiston, back to the realities of life.

It was a sad time when she left Whiston to return to her home in Oulton. Sad for two reasons, loss of her company and the realisation that another summer had passed by. It was time to prepare for another school year.

Aunty Louie suffered from a stroke in 1969 and died aged 81 - a sad loss to us.

A picnic across the common
Whiston

CHAPTER 13
An Ample Aunt

Another Aunt also visited Whiston - I can't remember her name or who she was related to. She made a big impression on me mainly because of her size which was.......... not to be rude let me say she was an ample, jolly person. She also seemed to be very well off as she wore expensive summer dresses with cardigans which had not been hand knitted.

I know it will sound as though I was always eating whilst at Dorothy's but I remember this ample aunt mainly for an elaborate picnic we had in the fields beyond the common, more or less where Aunty Louie and I would sit later in the summer.

Anyone who walks over Whiston Common and across the fields even today will notice the high sandstone walls with very narrow stiles formed from two upright slabs of stone. These are all very well for slim people to squeeze through, but oh dear! If you have a large frame, it is quite difficult, if not impossible, to pass through. This poor lady found very quickly that she was going to have considerable problems.

I got through, very easily as you would expect. Toby the dog got through as usual, but the Aunt got well and truly stuck, sideways. Although it seems rude the more she pushed and struggled, the more we laughed. She

saw the funny side of it and she was a determined woman who wasn't going to give in at the first stile! Her determination paid off and at last she got through by lifting herself up and over the top - no mean feat I can tell you. She was a good sport and we laughed together when we wondered how we were going to get her back again as it was steeper from the other side. Although there were other stiles which were equally impossible, we went out of our way to find gates which she found easier to make her way through.

The picnic we had was the best ever as it included sandwiches with salad, trifle, crisps with blue twists of salt, and a large bunch of grapes, which were only seen in Whiston normally when someone was very ill or in hospital - wonderful even if they were seeded. She also had a box of fancy cakes with fresh cream! Mmmmmm!

A picnic with the "ample" Aunt

So this meal, fit for a King was eaten beneath a clear blue sky under trees rather like those seen in 'Winnie the Pooh' illustrations, washed down with home made ginger beer.

When all was finished, we decided that rather than spoil her fine dress any more than it was already, we would make our way back by cutting through the wood and joining the lane from Moneystone, which comes out on the main road to Cauldon Lowe north of the Pinfold. It was quite a long walk, and I was most impressed by her stamina.

Looking back, I often wonder who she was, she left behind another glorious memory for me to look back on - Oh Happy Day!

CHAPTER 14
'Wingy Leese'

Whilst recollecting old Whiston characters, I must tell you about a man who Dorothy always referred to as 'Wingy Leese'.

At the age I was I did not understand that the name 'Wingy' was a nickname given to him years before. I said "Hello Wingy" to him when he passed by and he was most displeased especially with Dorothy who was embarrassed and hurried me on. I made her tell me why he was called 'Wingy Leese'. It appears that years previously the family had a feast at which a fowl had been eaten, a fact that he related to all his Whiston friends. "It were a wonderful fowl, it were," he said boasting "Me Mother had a wing, me Father had a wing, me Sister had a wing and I had a wing". Naturally the story of a fowl with four wings quickly spread around the district, which was two wings too many for the villagers who promptly bestowed on him the name of 'Wingy'. Nicknames like this were so very common then as most people from his generation had them, but this one I found the best I've heard in Whiston and illustrates the humour of the Moorlands.

I was only very young when I first heard of a village joke of 'Whiston Quarterpie' - "one half's tater, the other half's all tater!" I wonder who thought that one up?

CHAPTER 15
Sunday Teas and Chapel

Even though Dorothy had a very busy life keeping the house clean and tidy, the constant battle against weeds in the garden, peevish poultry and the needs of her Mother, she still found time in her life for her religion, being devoted to the local Methodist Chapel in Whiston.

Methodism had been practised in the village for many years. For all its small size, Whiston boasted two chapels from 1836, having both Wesleyan and Primitive Methodist followings. Both the chapels belonged to their Cheadle circuits each having visiting preachers each Sunday. The chapels were popular as there was no proper Church of England in Whiston until 1910, when stone taken from the demolished copper works in Black Lane was used to build one, saving a long walk to Kingsley which had been the Parish Church for centuries.

A new Primitive Methodist Chapel was built in 1908 with great celebrations in the village. Then in 1933 the Wesleyan and Primitives joined together, making the new chapel their joint place of worship.

Dorothy became treasurer of the Chapel which meant that the Ministers of Tean and the Circuit Superintendant from Cheadle visited quite often. They were treated with great reverence. A bright fire would be lit in the front room grate in his honour and tea served in the best china teacups and saucers. I would be told to keep quiet - or out of the way!

Whiston Chapel remains unchanged today, still a fine red-bricked building with large windows to let in the sunshine. It looks oddly cheerful in a rugged Moorlands village where stone-built dwellings are more in keeping than red brick. Whiston Chapel always feels friendly, never like a Victorian mausoleum as many chapels do, smelling of damp and mould. It had been in this chapel some years earlier that I had been christened with Dorothy standing as my God Mother, a fact which always made me feel a special attachment to her and perhaps she to me.

Records must have been badly kept at the chapel in the early 1950s, as the entry for my baptism is missing from the records. This omission was to cause me problems when I came to marry in 1972 and my baptism could not be found. Dorothy was able to swear as my Godmother that the act had actually taken place.

From a very young boy, I was sent to Sunday school at the chapel which was situated at the side of the chapel in a large room. I was taken there by my brothers and sisters where we all received a rudimentary Christian education. If I was to return I am sure that I would hear ghostly echoes of 'Climb Climb Up SunshineMountain' and 'Jesus Wants me for a Sunbeam'. I have been many things in my life but I don't think I have ever been a sunbeam, more of a cloudy day with scattered showers!

The chapel had to be cleaned on a rota basis, which, with only a small congregation, seemed to fall quite often on Dorothy. Dorothy would tie a headscarf around her head, don an old overall and set to work. There was no skimping, no just whisking a duster around. No, true to fashion everything was 'bottomed', and truly swept, polished and left gleaming with the wonderful smell of cedarwood. Chapel cleaning seemed to take hours and I would wander off, back down Ross Road, passing the house I was born in, re-living some of my younger years and memories in this pleasant country lane.

In the late afternoon with work finished and everything back in place, the key turned in the lock, it was time to walk back through Brookhollow, up the bank to Dorothy's and a cup of tea!

Dorothy rarely missed chapel on a Sunday evening, even on cold winters evenings when the cold icy fingers of the whistling wind would have been enough to keep most at home in front of a roaring fire. She had a simple faith, trusting in God, her maker, in a private manner which she rarely discussed. Armed with her flashlight, she would set out for chapel on a Sunday evening. Whiston, in those days had no street lighting and if there was no moon it would be pitch black except for the odd light in a house window. That's hard to imagine today when there are lights everywhere and orange pollution on the skyline!

Years ago, Dorothy's next door neighbour Mr. Ratcliffe, brother of Lizzie and of whom we will hear more later, was the organist. When he died he was succeeded by Mrs Annie Bull, Dorothy's cousin who lived at Cauldon Lowe just beyond Windy Harbour. She was a very likeable lady - no doubt still is - with a lovely smile and shiny red cheeks which made her look so healthy. She would often come for Sunday tea in the summer, before chapel. I liked her!

Sunday tea, in summer, was a special occasion over which Mrs Finney would preside with great ceremony - using the best tea service and the best cutlery with ivory handles. Sandwiches made from thinly sliced crusty bread, spread with butter and filled with home-baked ham if available or chopped ham and pork from a tin, or fresh tongue cooked and pressed by Dorothy and thinly sliced. But I still didn't care much for it as I could always see the great long tongue as the butcher brought it in his basket.

This was washed down with lots of tea. Fruit and cream would follow and finally cakes - a Victoria sponge with jam filling, dusted with icing sugar, seed cake and 'cut and come again' cake.

This meal was eaten very sedately in pleasant surroundings all wearing best clothes - ah, peace and contentment! Later it was off to chapel and the simple service of singing hymns, prayers, a sermon, collection and more hymns. A feeling of well being, a special day with a special ending - thanking God for his many blessings.

CHAPTER 16
The Mystery of the Pear

In the back field behind the house, next to the freshwater well, was a pear tree. Dorothy had quite a few fruit trees in the orchard but these were all damson and apple trees. A pear tree was a rarity in Whiston and it never had any fruit, year after year the pear tree existed in this way, no-one taking any notice of it at all. Whiston often suffers with late frosts which are devastating to the blossoms in late spring.

One year, lo and behold, a single blossom survived and began to develop, one solitary pear, but fascinating. The pear became an obsession. Everytime I visited I would run out to look at how the pear had grown since I last saw it. As the summer wore on the pear got very fat and in danger of falling. It looked yellow and juicy. I imagined sinking my teeth into this much watched pear and rather hoped that very soon I would.

One day in late summer I ventured out to see the pear........... - and it had gone. There was just a stalk hanging there, a space where the luscious fruit had been. I ran to the house immediately to enquire where it had gone. Blank faces met me, no-one owned up to devouring it. But I rather fancy that it disappeared into Dorothy's stomach!

Such are the disappointments of childhood!

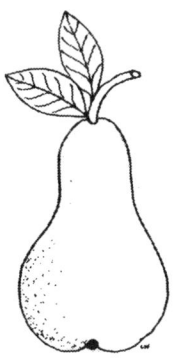

CHAPTER 17
A Tin of Treasure

On rainy days when the clouds closed in and hung lowly over the hillsides and the mist swirled around the common at Whiston, it was a time to stay indoors. But there was never any boredom at Dorothy's. Mrs Finney and I would usually spend the hours playing games and talking over old tales, but there were other times when she would take out her 'Treasure Tin' which had once held biscuits - many years ago since it had a picture of King Edward VII and Queen Alexandra in Coronation robes on it!

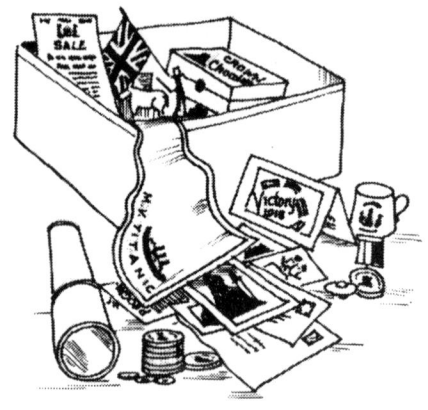

A tin of treasure

Inside this tin, which was much larger than a normal biscuit tin, were old medals, buttons, foreign coins and a half sovereign from Queen Victoria's reign - she had a top heavy crown which looked as if it would fall off her head. I had never seen a gold sovereign before. There were also farthings and silver threepenny bits which she called 'Joeys', I can't remember why! There were some of Dorothy's old tin toys; a clockwork monkey and a tin man who beat his mule with a stick, the mule then kicked back, knocking the man over! Here too was kept the sales catalogue of the Shrewsbury Sale at Alton Towers which she had attended in the 1920s.

There was also a souvenir napkin from the S.S.Titanic - everytime she took it out she would retell the story of the sinking of the great 'unsinkable' ship when it had hit an iceberg resulting in many deaths, including the Captain, a man named Smith who had been born in the nearby Potteries. A relation of Mrs Finney had travelled on the Titanic and had sent this souvenir to her when money was being raised to aid the survivors.

There was a photograph of her husband Jack, in the uniform of the Whiston Brass Band. He played the euphonium, which was still kept in a cupboard in Dorothy's room, but I was never allowed to handle it. She told me of a near miss with death when the Band were travelling on a boat which capsized on Rudyard Lake, north of Leek. Rudyard Lake was a great tourist

Whiston Brass Band 1925

attraction in those days and is well known for its under currents which have caused many deaths over the years in boating accidents. I can't remember all the details she told me of this disaster, perhaps someone else might!

Amongst all the many other interesting items in the old biscuit tin there were some American silver dollars, half dollars and early dimes. I collected old coins myself at that time, mainly Victorian pennies from 1860-1901 which were still in circulation. I recognised from Coin & Medal magazines that some American silver coins were quite valuable so took the advert up to Mrs Finney to see for herself. The coins were despatched to Spink & Co. of London, but I was never told how much they were worth in the end, but I would have loved to have known.

Also in the tin were postcards. Some were simple birthday greetings; others were used to announce that relatives would be visiting, others were from the Great War of 1914-18 which showed cartoons of Kaiser Bill and there were a few woven cards celebrating victory in 1918, showing the flags of the winning alliance. There were also photographs, some so faded it was hard to tell who the people were, standing so erect and with their stiff collars.

The treasure tin gave so much interesting fun, each piece a talking point, each with its own history and each a little part of Harriet's life.

CHAPTER 18
WASHDAY MONDAY

Wash day, which at Dorothy's was every Monday, was a day of hard work which began early at 5.30 am, often going on into late afternoon. It was a very necessary part of every Moorlands village life, repeated in all the households before the universal availability and affordability of the electric washing machine. It was, perhaps a part of the 'Good Old Days' into which modern technology would have been welcomed earlier by many a person with a large family.

So, washday came round each week, summer and winter, though summer washing was always easier of course than winter. At 5.30am, it was down into the wash-house in the cellars, open the creaking door, the clunk of the latch echoing loudly around the room. The damp coldness caused a shiver down your spine. In the far corner of the  dark blue-bricked wash-house with its white-washed walls was a large built-in washing boiler, known as the 'copper'. Under the copper boiler was a flue and fire grate. Water from the well was fetched whilst Dorothy got a roaring fire burning under the large boiler cauldron.

Many more trips would have to be made to the well to get water for rinsing. I was sure that my arms would stretch longer and longer. The rinsing tub was pulled down and made ready, along with the 'paunch' and 'dolly peg'. Dorothy would bring out the washing powder for the main wash, 'Lux' flakes for woollen garments which were hand-washed and a 'Dolly blue bag' which was used to make whites whiter, long before the 'miracle' of biological powders in the 1980s. There was also a box of Robin starch for stiffening the white cottons and it was liberally used.

Whilst the water was coming to the boil, the hens were let out and their breakfasts prepared and given to them. Our own breakfast, which was simple cereals with tea, was quickly consumed and the range fire lit ready for later in the day when it might be used to help dry the washing with the large clothes horses - also 'stabled' in the cellars.

Then the wash began in earnest, the whites bubbling away, before being rinsed in the large tub. Another tub was used to clean other clothes with the dolly peg twisting and turning the clothes in the tub in the hot soapy water - the same action as a modern washing machine's rotating action. These clothes were then rinsed.

Heavy washing was done with the 'paunch' which was a copper bell-like implement on a stail. It was hammered up and down on the washing, until you were worn out.

To be honest I can't remember all the stages of the washing, of what was washed with what and when starch was used or not. I just enjoyed the experience. The cellar wash-house was full of steam, water was slopped on the floor and all seemed like mayhem.

A 'modern' appliance was then rolled forward from a dark corner (I forgot to mention it before on your trip around the house). This was the mangle, hand operated, fun to use and good for building up muscles. It was used to remove as much water as possible from the washing before drying - it was made redundant by the invention of the spin-drier. It was great fun to turn the large handle round and round to turn the rollers. The washing was fed through the rollers which pressed the water out with great force. Very effective was a mangle!

Mangle

During the morning, Mrs Finney's breakfast had to be prepared and later a quick dinner taken of cold sliced roast beef left over from Sunday, with

cheese and pickles and a noggin' of bread, with plenty of hot tea to replace some of the fluids lost in perspiration! Then it was back on with the oilskin aprons and back downstairs to continue the wash. Soon pillow cases, sheets and all manner of washing was billowing out on the washing lines and the clothes horses were put to use. The water had to be emptied from the tubs and everything dried and put away and the floor mopped and dried. Soon all was back to normal again with the washing completed for another week - thank goodness.

This wasn't the end of it though. Naturally, all the washing had to be dried and then ironed. Dorothy had the use of an electric iron which was better than the old flat irons which had to be heated before the fire and was an art in itself I was told. The only person I ever saw using these heavy old Staffordshire irons was Mrs Spencer, a near neighbour. She used two irons, one was heated in front of her range whilst she used the other, and when this one cooled it was replaced with the hot one. There was an art in ironing as they had no thermostat to regulate the heat - the result could be scorching of the item being ironed. Mrs Spencer was still using these flat irons when I was married in 1972 and only had her first electric iron in 1973.

Dorothy's washing was whiter than white and smelled of ozone. It was something she was very proud of. A few years later she had an electric washer of her own and the mangle, rinsing tubs, paunch and dolly peg were all left redundant to become mere memories of the washday toil.

CHAPTER 19
LIZZIE'S

Jack and Lizzie Ratcliffe lived next door to Dorothy; I have mentioned them already. Being of a young age I had to refer to them as Mr Ratcliffe and Miss Ratcliffe, but we always referred to them as Lizzie and Jack out of Mrs Finney's earshot. I must admit to being frightened of Jack Ratcliffe, but there again I never remember ever having had a conversation with him. I imagine he was just a man who enjoyed his own privacy, maybe he was shy. I kept out of his way and all was fine.

I would have to pass in front of their house, very gingerly, to get to the steps which led up to another gate which brought you to the steep incline of the plain. It was a lovely walk up on the plain which came out on the top common. Dorothy had a right of way up the plain and down to the bridge below where it was possible to get through a stile onto Black lane. This right of way was sold to Tom Cooper I think when he was developing his golf course which also meant the Old Hall was brought back to life.

Mr Ratcliffe belonged to the generation of the sepia photographs of which Mrs Finney had a collection. He wore collarless shirts and a denim jacket and overall, especially when gardening. To give him credit, his garden was beautiful. It had every vegetable in season and not a weed in sight. He spent his retirement in his garden living with his sister in their 'house of wonders'. They rented their house from Harriet's sister Emma, who lived up at Windy Harbour, Upper Cotton.

Mrs Finney did not approve of Mr Ratcliffe for one reason, which involved the use of the washing stillage which each house had in the front garden wall. In the days when Victorian modesty still prevailed in certain Whiston households and virtue was a must, Jack Ratcliffe was frowned upon for his daring - each morning, summer and winter - to have a strip wash and shave in front of the house using the stillage to hold the enamelled bowl, water jug and shaving tackle. All this was done in full view of Mrs Finney and Dorothy which caused annoyance and much 'tut-tutting'. Personally, I couldn't see what the problem was but for the ladies, removing his shirt was just too much! But there he stood every morning in full view. Well, of anyone who might be peering through the windows, that is!

Lizzie Ratcliffe was a marvellous woman, rather like a bumbling mouse, with a heart of gold., very inoffensive, always trying to please. Using a broad Staffordshire dialect with no teeth made it hard to understand what she said but she always had a big smile and a gummy grin.

Lizzies house, although identical to Dorothy's in reverse, could not have appeared more different once you were inside the front door. The living room which was back to back with Dorothy's was dominated by a very large Victorian range, which was black leaded and housed an oven and hob. A large blackened kettle hung from a hook near the red glow of the fire andwas constantly simmering. Nearby an equally large brown teapot stood. It was only emptied once a day, I was told, with more tea thrown in liberally as required through the rest of the day! To say the obvious, the tea by the end of the day was very strong. My father used to enjoy it, he called it 'Roadman's Tea', the sort that you could stand your teaspoon up in!

Lizzie's was full of interesting antiques and other objects of fascination. A beautiful grandfather clock stood by the far wall but it had been let into the floor because the ceiling was too low for it to stand upright! There was a pair of very large Staffordshire Dogs, the biggest I've ever seen - they always had a mournful expression.

She had some lovely old china and furniture and a pair of pistols which, as they were the only ones I had ever seen at the time, immediately started my imagination thinking of highwaymen or who might have used them in some duel to the death! Lizzie also had some good pictures and very large religious oil prints which were very finely framed. Unlike next door everything seemed haphazard, but in a friendly relaxed way which was a reflection of Lizzie herself. I only saw the front or best room a couple of

The Staffordshire Pot Dog

times. It was typical of Moorlands front rooms, very tidy, not a thing out of place but rarely used - always kept for the special occasion that rarely happened.

After Jack Ratcliffe died, Lizzie lived on in the house alone but became increasingly dependent on Dorothy and other village help. She lived on for quite a few years. I can't remember her dying, it must have been in the early 1970s. I just hope that she remembered her teeth when she passed through the pearly gates!

CHAPTER 20
THE SAD TALE OF THE FOWL

When I was young, chicken was not the cheap, universal meat that it has become today. So when Dorothy gave my family a chicken which had outlived its usefulness, no longer laying eggs, it was most welcome.

One summer's day, after a Saturday spent in Whiston, I was asked to take a 'fowl' home for my Mother and Father. This was the only time this happened to me but it was once too many. The poor chicken, a lovely black one which was really plump did not like the idea of coming to Cheadle with me but had no choice. Dorothy caught hold of it and it squawked loudly before it was placed in a leather shopping bag with a zipper top. The zip was pulled across and I was assured that it would be no trouble. I wasn't convinced, but what could I do?

Dorothy carried it along Black Lane, across the Pinfold to the bus stop - no problems at all. Well it did shuffle about a bit but nothing too bad. We watched the bus coming into Whiston, past the chapel and the school and disappearing into the valley at Brookhollow, soon coming up the bank to where we were standing. I said "goodbye" to Dorothy, who crossed the road back to the Pinfold stile to wave. All buses had a conductor as well as a driver then, so I went halfway down the bus, which was quite full, and waved to her.

All was well. I paid the bus conductor my fare and he looked suspiciously at the bag which had soft sides, beginning to move as the chicken pushed against them. It then began to make a noise, then more noise. It suddenly took me by surprise by thrusting its head and neck through the small space between the side of the bag and the zip. What's more it now tried to get the rest of its body through the small space.

Panic! The struggling chicken

86

decided to make a shrieking noise. I tried to put its head back in, but it wouldn't go back. It was now causing a lot of attention. For two pins I would have unzipped the bag and let it free, but I didn't dare. The bus conductor came along with a grin on his face and rather like a policeman folded his arms and said "Hello, Hello, Hello, What have we got here then!" He decided to make a joke out of it. "Carrying livestock then are we?" he continued. Very worried and red as a beetroot, I sat petrified whist the stupid hen decided to peck at everything in sight. "We have to make a charge for livestock," he said getting out his fares book from inside his money bag. "Going to cost yer this is." I was nearly sick - my one dread was being put off the bus in the middle of the countryside, where I could be lost forever. I knew that I hadn't any money at all, my last few pennies had been spent on my bus fare.

The bus conductor must have seen my look of horror and distress - he tousled my hair and said "only joking lad" and went off up the bus. Phew! I was relieved. The chicken eventually decided to pull its own head back in and I held the ends of the bag top together until we, thankfully, pulled into Cheadle. The journey had seemed like a hundred miles at least! The poor chicken now seemed resigned to its fate. I wasn't at all happy at being the one to bring it to its end and I tried to put it out of my mind when the roast chicken was put on the table, brown, plump and steaming!

Thankfully, this never happened again, else I may have become a vegetarian well before I did!

Growing up in Forsbrook

CHAPTER 21
ANOTHER TRIP TO WHISTON

As there was no direct bus to Whiston other than on Wednesday, Friday and Saturday, if I wanted to get to Dorothy's on other days, I would catch a bus from Cheadle to Froghall in the Churnet Valley and walk up the steep Whiston Bank into Leys Heath and the village. It always seemed a long walk but young legs find it fairly easy and the traffic was very light then with far less lorries which now make it so dangerous.

The railway runs through Froghall, past the copper works. From the road bridge it was possible to overlook the railway station and watch any train coming up the valley from Uttoxeter. Steam trains have always fascinated me and it was quite rare for me to see one. One fine summer's morning I jumped off the bus at Froghall very quickly as I could see a plume of white smoke coming up the valley. Sure enough a full train soon pulled into the station below.

Froghall Staion

As it began to move forward towards the bridge, I crossed the road and put my head over the bridge to watch the engine go right underneath. I got the shock of my life when clouds of hot smoke belched right into my face. I coughed, spluttered and tasted a vile taste in my mouth. My face and shirt were dotted with black smuts!

Luckily no-one was around to see my silly trick and I quickly left Froghall behind and began the serious climb of the steep incline up through the beautiful woodlands which curtain the valley. Near the top of the bank lived the Hitchen family in a long cottage which has now been demolished. Mrs Hitchen's son Robert was a school friend of my brother's and I also knew their daughter Margaret from Whiston school days and had visited their house on occasions.

If ever I walked up the bank, Mrs Hitchen would be leaning over the gate with a big smile. I would stop to take a breather and if I was lucky she would give me a drink, which on a hot summer's morning was most welcome. Just around the corner from here it is possible to climb through the trees and join the Plain by going through an arch in a house built over the old rail track. This cut off the Leys Heath corner. The end of this track brought you to the main road which was crossed again following the old rail bed into Whiston.

Just below here lived another old Whiston couple Mr & Mrs Myatt who lived in what was then a fairly modern red-bricked house set in a large garden. The garden was tended by their son Jim. The Myatts had two unmarried daughters who worked at the Boltons copper works. They were named Gladys and Doris. We used to call them Morris and Doris after two mice from a story. When I was very young I sometimes visited Mrs Myatt with my mother. She would always be sitting by the fire and would talk in her warm rather nasally Staffordshire voice - she would call me a 'Rumptyfizzer' which I did not know what to make of!

Walking on, I was soon passing the Village Garage owned by Mr Keene and looking down on the house I was born in, wishing we had never left. Then on past the chapel and church and pausing to look at the school where I had spent my happy formative years. I remembered Mrs Wilson the headmistress who used to roar into Whiston on her motorbike and Mrs Rogers my teacher who encouraged me so much.

It was then down to Brookhollow and up the bank to Dorothy's just in time for a welcome drink and another idyllic day.

The climb out of Brookhollow, up Black Lane towards Ivy Cottage

Opposite the Pinfold was the bus stop for the return to Cheadle on Saturdays

CHAPTER 22
A WINTER BONUS

In winter the weather can quickly change in the Moorlands. It could be raining in Cheadle and snowing in Whiston. It was always a hope of mine that there would a fall of sufficient snow on a winter's day visit to ensure that the local bus service would be cancelled - and that I would be stranded in Whiston.

Needless to say this rarely happened - in fact in all the years this only happened once, but I made the most of it! I would have been ten years old when it did. If I remember rightly there was no threat of snow, otherwise I would have been kept safely at home in Cheadle. By dinner time a strong wind from the east was bringing in the showers of snow. Looking out of the bedroom window of Mrs Finney, I saw the rest of the village quickly obscured in grey swirling clouds.

Silent wishes, please keep snowing. Wish answered - more and more snow! Although Dorothy and I went to wait for the bus it became very obvious that it was not going to get up the banks to Whiston. I kept telling myself and Dorothy that the bus wasn't coming. I wanted to start back to her house in case it did finally make it! We trudged back from the Pinfold where I caught the bus, home to Dorothy's where I was given a pair of rather large sized wellingtons to wear and then it was down the Slippery Lane to Brook Hollow to the phone box next door to the shop to phone my father at Cheadle Hospital where he worked.

For all the cold which bit through my coat and froze my ungloved hands there was an overriding sense of excitement at the coming adventure. Into the telephone box which allowed the ears to warm a little, then clunk, clunk, clunk, clunk of the four pennies into those old boxes with their A and B buttons to press. The heavy bakelite receiver was lifted to her ear andI could hear a familiar voice on the other end.

In common with many people Dorothy hated having to make telephone calls and always handled them as if they would bite, given half the chance. She would hold the receiver well away from her ear and shout her message down the mouth piece in a high pitched matter-of-fact voice which is amusing to recollect. Her face would look worried until the ordeal was over.

It was settled then, I was to stay until the snow abated and my father would fetch me in his car. Great!

The heavy receiver was replaced, clunk, and feeling marooned we visited Wordleys shop for a few things she needed and a bar of '5 Boys' chocolate for me.

It was then back to Dorothy's and all the evening jobs were finished as rapidly as possible. The hens were on their perches early so that wasn't too bad. The snow by now was whistling around the house and sticking to the sandstone walls and climbing up the doors - time to finish for the day and get

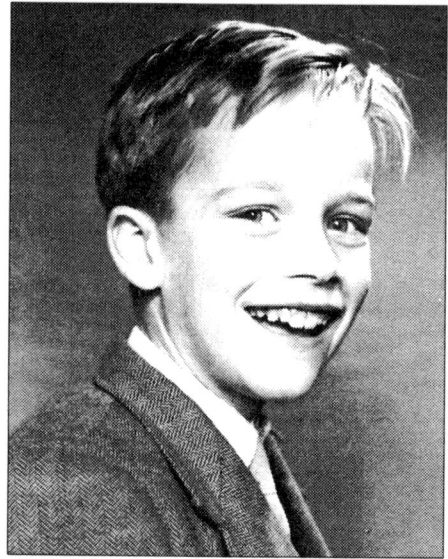

Happy days

in front of the crackling fire, bolt the doors and enjoy the isolation. Toby went to his 'corner' and Toosey the cat went under the couch which was a warm place to be. It was down to the cellar to find some large potatoes, which after being scrubbed, pricked with a fork, placed on a tin dish in a little water and liberally sprinkled with salt, disappeared into the hot range oven, especially stoked up for the evening!

This was a meal worth waiting for, baked potatoes with lashings of butter, home-cured bacon dripping with tasty dip, pickled onions and beetroot chutney with a sprinkling of salt. To think of eating this meal with the wind whistling around the house, a flickering light and the warm glow of the range brings a satisfying memory to me now. Dorothy had a set of ancient (or so they seemed to me) cutlery. The forks had only two very sharp prongs, instead of normal' forks I had ever used. They made eating peas and suchlike quite difficult to handle, as you can imagine.

After drawing hot water and washing up in the tin bowl, it was up to Mrs Finney's room - she had been having one of her 'bad do's' which meant she would not venture downstairs. With the awful draughts which were coming from every direction that night I can't say that I blame her. The next couple of hours were spent with Mrs Finney, telling her Whiston Eaves yarns and then playing card games and draughts. We looked through the enormous family bible which had beautiful colour plates such as Moses parting the Red Sea and Ruth gleaning in the fields which I still picture in my mind.

MOSES IN THE LAND OF THE MIDIAN

I normally had to go to bed quite early - unnecessarily early to my mind - so at Dorothy's it was good to be allowed to stay up much later than at home! Going to bed on a cold winter's night in a house which creaked and groaned and set the imagination running riot, gave me a shiver down my spine. However, there was no way I was going to let Dorothy see I was the least bit scared, so everything had to be braved!

At Dorothy's they had a very novel way of warming the beds which I have to admit was better than water bottles. Enormous pebbles were placed in the oven and heated right through for several hours, they were then wrapped in covers and put into the beds. They were really warm all night. They were great unless you stubbed your toes against one or dropped one on your foot!

I was then supposed to have a wash which was a little daunting when you consider that it had to be done in the cellar with so many dark shadows and imagined mice and rats lurking behind the barrels. However, as I said, Dorothy wasn't the sort of person who understood being scared, so it was down those steps into the echoing cellar with a hot pitcher of water. The washing bit was carried out as quickly as possible - what she might call a 'cat lick' - vigorously drying with a rough towel, then rushing back up the steps and back to the warm fire! Feeling a little guilty at the speed in which the whole operation was carried out, I faced the questioning look from Dorothy - the unspoken question, have you had a GOOD wash? The evening was rounded off with a mug of 'Bournvita' which was a treat I didn't get at home.

A winter's view of Whiston Hall. On the left is what used to be Stoniers' shop.

Getting into bed was another icy experience, the shock of cold sheets and the searching with the feet for the hot pebbles. But before this I climbed into the deep window to look outside. The snow had stopped, although the wind remained and a clear sky was lit up by an enchanting full moon, which shone down on Whiston Village below, silent and sleeping. Thousands of stars twinkled in that sky.

A beautiful charcoal picture of Nellie, Dorothy's dog prior to Toby, looked down on me from the wall beside the bed which made me feel safe. Then the light went out and I was enveloped in darkness with the wind still howling around the house roof.

The next morning, rushing to the window revealed that the snow, so menacing the evening before, was already thawing with a faint clear blue sky which gave the promise of a better day to come - and collection by my Father.

The memory of that snowy winters night in Whiston has remained with me ever since.

CHAPTER 23
THE SPENCERS OF NORTH VIEW

Mr & Mrs Spencer lived at North View, just down the lane from Dorothy's. North View was a brick house built sometime just after 1910, built onto the corner of Stone Cottage after the demolition of the copper works. I imagine it was called North View because the only view the house had was north - and that from the bedroom windows overlooking the old waste spoil heaps to the fields beyond. The house hadn't changed since it was built, having no modern conveniences until the early 1970s.

Mrs Spencer was a really jolly, colourful Moorlands character who always had not only a smile but a very infectious laugh which made her shake from head to toe. This was always noticeable when she made her weekly trip to Cheadle Market for her weeks shopping in town. Her laugh could be heard echoing all down the bus if something amused her.

During the day she would wear a cross-over pinafore and an Ena Sharples' hair net which made her look rather like Beatrix Potters' Mrs Tiggywinkle, especially as she had an ample figure. As you can see, Mrs Jenny Spencer was not an easy person to forget. She lived with her husband, Eric, who worked at Thomas Boltons copper works in nearby Froghall. She was an exceptionally good cook. She had learned her skills at Farley Hall, when it was the home of the Bill Family. This is where she met Eric who was working nearby. They fell in love and eventually married, living happily together.

Eric Spencer was a very thoughtful, practical man, full of old country wisdom, slow and pondering. He always gave good advice whether you wanted it or not. He told his stories so slowly that by the time he had finished, it was easy to have forgotten the beginning. What made it worse was that Mrs Spencer would start telling you a story of her own half way through his! It was very difficult at times.

He suffered with a very bad chest and could not breathe too easily, especially as his life wore on. He was always absolutely sure that he would not live a day over the allotted time as quoted in the Bible - three score years and ten, 70. He was most surprised when he did!

The Spencers had a good collection of old Whiston photographs and unusual curios including two glass walking sticks - most odd! They were very proud of the fact that they had been able to save 2s 6d a week ever since their marriage.

Unusually for Whiston, the Spencers garden was not very large at all but Eric had a garden shed and enjoyed his patch of garden to the full. One of the things Eric enjoyed planting was his yearly bean row. Bean rows are a phenomenon in Moorlands gardens - or used to be, an absolute must along with rhubarb, which suited the acidic soil.

The bean row was inspected daily, as the bean plants raced up the poles and flowered their bright red flowers indicating how good the crop might be. The runner beans would then grow, longer and longer until they were ready to harvest over a longish period, when beans would be constantly on the menu. As there was no freezer available, other ways of preserving beans for the winter were used. The most successful was when they were 'put down' for the winter in very large glass jars. Salt bought in large blocks was crushed and used in layers - a layer of salt and a layer of beans - repeated until the jar was full. Several of these jars were filled and stored in the pantry, along with all the pickles and jams which were also staples for the winter.

Not only did Mrs Spencer make jam, pickles and chutney but she also made raspberry vinegar, an ideal remedy for colds. She also stored apples, cooking apples and pears in her cold store. It meant that during the winter months there would be supplies of fruit throughout. I suppose this is how it had been done for centuries before the coming of the chest freezer and the availability of fruit and vegetables all year round whatever the home season. The beans were brought out in winter, taken out of their salty store, washed in clean water and left to soak overnight, then cooked the next day. They were a little too salty for my taste but they were a welcome treat in winter, making a change from the other staple grown in their garden - brussel sprouts!

The bean row was then a very important part of the Moorlands garden and woe betide if anything went wrong with it. After I was married, we became neighbours of the Spencers, who were super neighbours. We called round one summer's morning following a night of high winds and torrential rain storms. High winds are not uncommon in Whiston at anytime of year, but this one had been particularly rough. We went into the Spencer's living room. Mr. Spencer had his head in his hands and Mrs Spencer sat at her table staring into space with a fixed expression. We were immediately concerned that someone close to them had perhaps died. When we enquired as to their melancholy state we were told that the night before the ferocious wind had blown down and completely destroyed the hallowed bean row!

What can one say to someone who has lost a bean row? Many other bean rows in the area had also been destroyed by that wind. It was rather like the potato blight in the 1840s. There were no beans that winter for sure!

Mrs Spencer was a good housekeeper, very tidy and, like Dorothy, very proud of the whiteness of her washing. The house had a beautiful range in an Art Nouveau style in cream with red flowers. They had it ripped out in the early 1970s replacing it with a tiled grate. The walls were painted dark brown half way and cream the other half with a picture rail near the top of the wall.

The Spencers had only gas laid on until 1972, when we gave permission

(which the previous owner had denied them) for electricity to be taken over our own property to their house. This transformed the Spencer's whole life. She could now have a washer, a fridge, a television and an electric iron. The electric irons replaced the flat irons which I used to watch being used by her when I was a lad.

The best room or 'parlour' was only used on Sundays which is common even today in the Moorlands. Jenny Spencer was very proud of the harmonium which was kept in the best room. She played her harmonium and sang sweetly too and although neither of them were regular church goers she could sing and play hymns as well as anyone.

In their younger days they used to take trips out at weekends and they enjoyed going to watch motorbike racing, taking a picnic lunch with them.

When they had a television they became addicts and looked out their old blackout curtains which had been kept from the Second World War, blacking out the daylight so that they could watch without the light from the sun ruining the picture quality.

Now they have both passed away, Whiston has lost two of its characters.

A picture of Mrs Spencer in 1973, taken outside
Willow Cottage. She is with my wife Rosamund and
our black cat named Mitten

CHAPTER 24
CHRISTMAS MEMORIES

I remember with affection Christmas at Dorothy's which was celebrated in a simple no frills way, but very satisfying.

Christmas Eve was the time for the delivering of cards and presents by my Mother and Father which, of course, included old friends at Whiston. Sharing Christmas Eve with other people, wishing 'Happy Christmas' to all you met, heightened the anticipation of Christmas Day itself. Whiston was the evening destination, calling with a card to Mr & Mrs Sam Keene at Whiston Garage, then into Ross Road to our old neighbours next door to where I was born, Mr & Mrs Walker and their son Andrew, who was a similar age to me. Cards would be posted to other neighbours including the Allen family.

Then it was off to Dorothy's with presents and a card which were well received. My Father had been a good friend of Jack Finney and had sat with him for hours during his last illness.

For the Christmas season, Dorothy would bring in holly with lots of red berries and she would decorate all the pictures and mirrors. The ceilings were too low to have garlands but she would either have a small spindly tree decorated with baubles and a fairy, or the branch of a fur similarly decorated as part of a table decoration. Cards were hung from ribbons in lines across the walls.

Dorothy loved Christmas, the presents, cards and anticipation. She would be preparing the cake and puddings in October and the beetroot chutney in November. Her puddings were much prized presents which were made using the finest ingredients and boiled for hours wrapped in muslin. As well as a pudding, she would give a jar of her famous beetroot chutney and a jar of picked onions - what better present could you ask for at Christmas?

I always tried to give Dorothy a good Christmas present which meant saving pocket money for weeks, but it was always appreciated. But I never saw her open a present as we always made her promise not to open any of her presents until Christmas Day.

I would also pop round to Lizzies next door with something small for her. She was so pleased that she had been remembered too.

Unless illness intervened, Dorothy and her Mother would travel up to Windy Harbour each year to spend Christmas Day with Dorothy's Aunty Emma, year after year!

After I was married, it became a tradition for Rosamund and I to visit on Christmas Eve to both the Spencers and Dorothy to deliver presents. It always brought back the feeling of the excitement of Christmas Day coming - Christmas pudding and the chutney and the onions would be gratefully received. All would be set for the big day!

We would be invited back to Whiston to have a Christmas Tea with Dorothy and her Mother, which was a treat not to miss. I think I enjoyed it best when it was on a Sunday when following the delicious tea we could accompany Dorothy to chapel. There's nothing like singing Christmas carols in a Methodist chapel! Tea would be prepared and eaten in the living room in front of a roaring fire. However you will remember me talking about the cold draughts - well they got no better, so unless you were lucky enough to sit near the fire it was rather cold on your back.

The drop leaf table would be brought out, covered with a starched, white embroidered tablecloth. The best rosebud china teaset would be used with the best cutlery. Sandwiches were prepared and placed on the sandwich tray in a long line and the Christmas cake placed in the middle of the table. It always had thick marzipan with white and pink icing.

Sandwiches were accompanied by the famous beetroot chutney, pickled onions and slices of tomatoes, lots of hot tea, Christmas cake, mince pies and if that wasn't enough, cheesecake. Enough to make you groan - but worth it I assure you!

It's very pleasing that our daughter, Lydia, was able to join in this Whiston Christmas celebration, so it's part of her memories too - and something we miss now very much as each Christmas comes around. Mrs Finney presented Lydia with Dorothy's Christmas Fairy which would sit precariously on top of the spindly tree. It is now unwrapped very carefully each year when the season arrives, bringing back Christmas memories of Whiston.

Oulton in the early 1900s. The home of the Malpasses
On the left below, Rosamund on a donkey and on the right with her parents

CHAPTER 25
A MEETING OF DESTINY

One sunny summer's morning, I caught the bus bound for Leek Market via Oakamoor and Whiston. It was 1959 and I was eight years old. My Mother had seen me safely onto the bus in Cheadle and I was off for another days adventure at Dorothy's. The journey passed well enough and eventually after the seemingly long journey, I was soon alighting at Whiston, Brookhollow.

It was very rare that anyone else ever got off the bus at Whiston, so I was curious when two grown-ups, a girl and a baby in a carrycot got off the bus behind me. They were strangers to Whiston, I was sure of that! I ran on ahead up the bank towards Ivy Cottage and then looked back as I usually did to admire the view - the strangers were following in my footsteps up the bank. Deciding not to hang around, I ran on up the hill towards Stablehouse well ahead of the strangers, I even braved the dogs, barking loudly as usual but not biting. luckily I survived the dogs and at the top of the hill by the outbuildings opposite Stoniers Shop I looked again - they were still following.

Going on ahead I lost them for a while until they rounded the corner to Dorothy's. Up the track I went, through the green gate, greeted by a boisterous Toby as usual and not pausing I ran to the door, knocked and was let in.

Out of breath, I quickly related the story of the strangers following and Dorothy laughed. This day I was not to be the only visitor, the strangers were in fact Dorothy's relations from Oulton - Aunty Louie's niece, her husband and daughters. Rather disappointed and apprehensive I melted into the background when they knocked on the door. A great deal of fuss was made and the kettle made ready for a cup of tea. A fire had been lit in the front room and they disappeared into there. The girl I was told was named Rosamund, she was a year younger than me. She called Mrs Finney, Aunty Harriet.

I was asked to show her around, but as first was not too happy at having a girl to share my own little world. Harriet had made a big effort today and was up and ready, talking ten to the dozen. 'Visiting Aunty Harriet' was something which relations only did after giving notice of their intentions well in advance of the day. She was considered very weak and everyone had to be careful so as not to give her a heart attack through 'shock' and excitement. In reality she outlived nearly all her contemporary relatives and even her own daughter Dorothy!

Being brought out of hiding and very shy as I wasn't keen on strangers, I was introduced as Reg Williams' lad from Cheadle. It was obvious that they were going to be involved in a heavy days talking, in the way grown-ups tend to do, with much clucking and pampering of the new baby, named Christine.

Dorothy asked me to show the girl, Rosamund, the hens and around the top end of Whiston. Although I was still feeling resentful at these relations who were visiting on MY day, I decided to make the most of it; besides the girl seemed quite affable. I took her all around my favourite haunts, I took her in the cellar and we took some corn out for the hens and went looking for eggs, although it was too early in the day really. Up the back field we went up to the back wall, which we climbed up to view the black sheet of water which was the bottomless pit and the tunnel which took the track from the Hall Farm under the Plain to the fields on the other side.

After looking around the garden and the cornfield with its central tree which we climbed a short way up, we went off to the Top Shop for some sweets. Having looked at everything at Dorothy's, I thought that I would show her all my haunts on the common and the big rock in the next field. We went back to the house for Toby as I thought that it would be a good idea to take him with us as he loved the exercise. The day had gone cloudy and a drizzle was threatening but damp weather was something we often put up with in Whiston so we weren't put off.

Rosamund insisted that she be allowed to hold Toby on his lead across the common. The cheek of it! There was no way I was going to allow this as it was MY job to do that. So, this then was our first row which didn't last too long as Dorothy intervened and insisted that Rosamund be allowed to take him on the trip out and I would bring him back! How's that for compromise? Over the heather covered common we went, firstly peering over the black ring wall of the Hall, sharing my conjectures as to the tragedy of thwarted love which had left its windows blocked to the daylight, protected only by the rooks soaring and wheeling above.

Rosamund shared her sweets with me, so perhaps she wasn't so bad after all. We squeezed through the stone pillars of the stile in the gritstone wall into the green field beyond and onto the large slab of rock which had to be climbed each time I passed it. Of course, I helped Rosamund to climb it, although to be honest I never had a good head for heights but I wasn't going to let her know that as I soon found out she climbed better than me! We walked on to the woods and Whiston Barn before returning, as we were both feeling hungry. As we got back to Dorothy's the drizzle was now turning to rain, such a shame as we were now both enjoying each other's company. In the afternoon we played together in the front room including Lions and Tigers on all fours fighting and eating each other!

Later the weather brightened and we were able to feed the hens and collect the eggs together. I had my wellingtons but Rosamund got really muddied up, which Dorothy wasn't very pleased about, especially the white ankle socks which were now brown! Somehow I got the blame for it! We had an afternoon tea together and were by now firm friends.

Soon, too soon, it was time to get ready to catch the bus back to Cheadle as it returned back through the villages from Leek. I knew that we were both wishing that the bus wouldn't come; perhaps we would mistime it. We stood at the Pinfold, crestfallen, watching the road ahead for the red bus which surely would appear very shortly. We waited and waited but no bus appeared. We were so pleased. In the end we walked to Brookhollow with Dorothy to ring my father to see if he would

The corner of grass still known as the pinfold although this feature of village life has long disappeared from Whiston

come and fetch us after he finished work. Of course he agreed, but it would be two and a half hours before we would see him. We enjoyed the extra time together. Mrs Finney, known as Aunty Harriet to Rosamund remarked "Those two were meant for each other" with a knowing smile which embarrassed me. Dorothy cut her short replying "Be quiet Mother -

matchmaking".

My Father arrived at half past six and took us up to Oulton where Rosamund lived and we said "Goodbye" to each other.

We did keep in touch, always sending birthday, Christmas and Valentine cards! We saw each other on other visits but not often. Years later, however, we did find each other and quite fittingly began our married life together in Whiston.

Rosamund with Toby on the Upper Plain, above Mrs Finney's

CHAPTER 26
TIME & LIFE MOVE ON

The years roll by so very quickly, even Dorothy's changed in the early 1970s leaving some of the hard times behind, very thankfully for her. The old outbuildings were demolished, including the old store shed where the old wheelbarrow and the scythes were kept and the pig styes where I knocked my head looking for eggs, and the shed where some of the fowl roosted.

A new extension was added with bathroom, inside toilet and spacious kitchen with sink unit and cooker. The old front room became the new living room with a new doorway leading to the cellar steps. The old living room became the best room. It was goodbye to the faithful old range which had served so well, ripped out and replaced with a tiled fireplace. The cellar doorway was blocked up and the floor of red and black tiles carpeted - no more scrubbing the floor on hands and knees with the soft soap scrubbing brush and steaming water.

Gone were the old paned windows, replaced with single panes, easier to clean but with less character. All the old washing equipment became redundant, no trips back and forth to the well to fetch the cold sparkling spring water; goodbye to the dolly tub and dolly peg, the paunch and the washing boiler with all the aching muscles too after a hard days wash!

A driveway was made through the old orchard and the large wooden water vat was chopped up for firewood. The old classical head disappeared from the washing stillage for fear it would be stolen, but leaving the shells which let you hear the mighty roar of the sea when you put them to your ear.

Lizzie, next door, grew frail and eventually passed on to a better life. Then the coming of the golf course was to change the Whiston of my childhood. The common was tamed, the Old Hall received new life with shining windows, cars now trundled up the drive over the common and greens appeared where I used to play. The top shop closed and new dwellings began filling in the spaces through the village, eating away at the small fields bordering Black lane and Brookhollow.

The inclined plain through the gate past Lizzie's house was partially removed, again for the golf course. One good thing to happen was the old copperworks tips were re-shaped which improved the look of the village from the main road.

Yes, all was change. I changed too as the years rolled by, a new school, new friends, a move from Cheadle to Forsbrook. New responsibility when my father took over a grocery business at Cheadle's Townend, helping in the shop and delivering orders with my older brother David.

I still visited Dorothy when I could, but the long summer days of my carefree boyhood had sadly passed by.

Toby the dog who had been my companion on so many adventures grew old and died to be replaced by a Jack Russell, whom Dorothy called Romp. I never took to Romp as I had Toby but I have a picture of him as a pup.

It was the last time I was to stay at Dorothy's for a whole week, joined by my brother Ken. The year was 1969 and I was 18 years old. The last time I washed in the cold cellar bringing back the feelings experienced years before, perhaps a sadness that everything now seemed so much smaller and the wonder of childhood was laid to rest. I was now an adult.

Dorothy gained more freedom in later years through the close friendship of the Cotton family and her cousin Derek from Cheadle. Dorothy's health began to suffer and she was saddened by the death of her close cousin John Bull who died of cancer. Then Dorothy became ill with cancer herself. It was a difficult time. I sat with her one day when she was ill in her bed and we talked about how she had helped make my growing years, when I had visited her, so good. It made her smile even though she was in great pain. Dorothy died in the Douglas MacMillan Home in 1989 with Harriet soldiering on until 1990 aged 94.

I sincerely hope that you, the reader, have enjoyed my reflections of my young days in Whiston.

The House on the Plain

on
the Plain

A Whiston History

by

John Williams

Published by

CHURNET VALLEY BOOKS

43 Bath Street
Leek
Staffordshire
01538 399033

© John Williams
and Churnet Valley Books
1997

ISBN 1897949 26 X

Printed in Great Britain by The Ipswich Book Company, Suffolk.